Praise for
Abolitionist Intimacies

El Jones has gifted us all with a political beacon for liberation and an ethical compass for how to be. This stunning book is a powerful narration of how abolitionist futures are built in the present — through Black feminist abolitionist intimacies of witnessing, relationality, organizing, communing, and co-resistance. *Abolitionist Intimacies* is a searingly lyrical, poignant, and revolutionary must-read; an absolute tour de force that I cannot recommend highly enough.

— Harsha Walia, author of *Undoing Border Imperialism*
and *Border and Rule*

Abolitionist Intimacies is an urgently needed text. Drawing from years of organizing experience, Jones's work as a Black feminist theorist, activist, and scholar skillfully draws attention to the banal violence of carcerality in Canada and the ongoing work of freedom-oriented struggle. With rigour, theoretical agility, and a grounded sense of integrity, Jones forwards a poetic vision of intimacy, care, and human liberation, sketching out abolitionist futures beyond policing, prisons, and cages.

— Robyn Maynard, author of *Policing Black Lives*,
co-author of *Rehearsals for Living*

Through poetry, song, memos, journalism, and academic essays informed by the Black feminist tradition and years of work with criminalized and illegalized people, *Abolitionist Intimacies* makes visible the many injustices of the present while articulating a vision for a caring future free from state, corporate, and interpersonal violence. From cover to cover, El Jones shares a creative approach to abolitionist critique and praxis that, intervention by intervention, works to dismantle and build alternatives to carcerality in the lives of human beings that are targets of structural and interpersonal violence fuelled by white supremacy, racism, sexism, heterosexism, capitalism, and ableism. This book is a must-read for those seeking a clear picture of how the Canadian carceral state operates; the devastating impacts of its laws, institutions, policies, and practices on people and communities pushed to the margins; and what is possible when we come together to collectively resist and build alternative ways of relating to each other to produce real safety and liberation.

— Justin Piché, Associate Professor of Criminology at the University of Ottawa and editor of the *Journal of Prisoners on Prisons*

A powerful collection of poetry, political analysis, and personal reflection from an inspiring scholar-activist who connects mind, heart, body, and soul to express the meaning of abolition in so-called Canada. El Jones takes her reader from the kitchen table to the prison waiting room, from Angela Davis to Idle No More, from grief to rage to "joyous loudness." Refusing to gloss over the complexity of building solidarity against racism, colonialism, patriarchy, and capitalism, El Jones takes time to linger in those moments of intimacy and care that sustain movements for collective liberation. A must-read for anyone who wants to remember what it means to be human in the face of systemic violence.

— Lisa Guenther, Queen's National Scholar of Political Philosophy and Critical Prison Studies, Queen's University, and author of *Solitary Confinement: Social Death and Its Afterlives*

Abolitionist Intimacies is not only an act of resistance but an act of care. In the context of the prison industrial complex and what Jones calls "carceral intimacies" enacted through coercive power and abuse, El Jones offers the counter-practice of abolitionist intimacies, characterized by love, care, healing, forgiveness — insurgent acts within and outside prison walls.

Throughout this book, author and poet El Jones generously articulates what it means to engage in ideas of intimacies by articulating their relationship to state violence at different carceral sites, from prisons to borders, from hospitals to social work. She reminds us: abolition is a global project that includes the fight against militarization, homelessness, poverty, and gender-based violence.

El Jones takes the project of abolition away from institutions and academia and back to grassroots organizing by centring the voices of victims of state violence. She reminds us that prisoners and victims are not separate people and prison abolition is indeed a feminist issue. El

Jones turns to living archive, recovering what is lost, erased, and buried, by refusing to forget those we have lost to state violence, to prisons, to banishment. She argues that abolitionist praxis can't be limited to a theoretical act but must be supported by actions towards our collective liberation.

Abolitionist Intimacies responds to the urgent need for abolitionist literature centred on the Canadian prison as a colonial, white supremacist project. *Abolitionist Intimacies* is an immensely generous contribution to Black feminist abolitionist literature in Canada and to living in abolitionist relationship to the world. As a Black feminist engaged in abolition work in so-called Canada, I see this book recognizing the value of abolition work in spaces beyond academia, where abolition organizing happens every day, particularly created and nurtured by the labour of Black women. This type of abolition work lives in our communities every day and manifests through our refusal to forget, to banish, or dehumanize those confined to prison walls.

Abolitionist Intimacies is a gift of love and care. Abolition work must be truly directed at, produced for, and done with folks who are incarcerated; it must manifest in the ways we resist and ways we overcome.

— Marlihan Lopez, co-ordinator at the Simone de Beauvoir Institute
and co-founder of the Defund the Police Coalition in Montreal

Abolitionist Intimacies

Abolitionist Intimacies

EL JONES

Fernwood Publishing
Halifax & Winnipeg

Development editing and copyediting: Fazeela Jiwa
Cover design: Evan Marnoch
Design and layout: Brenda Conroy

Printed and bound in Canada

Published by Fernwood Publishing
2970 Oxford Street, Halifax, Nova Scotia, B3L 2W4
and 748 Broadway Avenue, Winnipeg, Manitoba, R3G 0X3
fernwoodpublishing.ca

Fernwood Publishing Company Limited gratefully acknowledges the financial support of the Government of Canada through the Canada Book Fund and the Canada Council for the Arts. We acknowledge the Province of Manitoba for support through the Manitoba Publishers Marketing Assistance Program and the Book Publishing Tax Credit. We acknowledge the Province of Nova Scotia through the Publishers Assistance Fund and Arts Nova Scotia.

Library and Archives Canada Cataloguing in Publication
Title: Abolitionist intimacies / by El Jones. Names: Jones, El, 1979- author.
Description: Poems and prose. Includes bibliographical references and index.
Identifiers: Canadiana (print) 20220253218 | Canadiana (ebook) 20220253900 | ISBN 9781773635521 (softcover) ISBN 9781773635736 (EPUB) | ISBN 9781773635743 (PDF)
Classification: LCC PS8619.O5324 A76 2022 | DDC C811/.6—dc23

I dedicate this book to all incarcerated and formerly incarcerated people. I wrote to honour all who have lost their lives in this country's carceral institutions and all who have lost their lives after release due to neglect, lack of resources, ongoing trauma, and systemic violence, including the criminalization of drugs.

I remember the words of a young incarcerated man who told me, "one way or another, we all will be released." May that release come through freedom, and may we continue to fight for liberation and a world where prisons no longer exist.

Destruction

A LOVE POEM

There's a statue of your rapist
Overlooks the square where people gather
And high up on the hill
There's a plaque
To the men who shot your father
And the knowledge of their deeds
It just pass through them like water
So another generation
Learns from them to rape your daughter

I heard you moved onto a street
Named for men who led the slaughter
And when you begged to take it down
They told you go sit in the corner
And they say their speech is sacred
And yours just never matters
So the boot heel of the past
Will crush your throat
Forever after

But if you go get the ropes
I'll bring the bulldozer
Because what we learned from our history
Is how quick their idols shatter
And they taught us how to wipe away
And end the day in laughter
Like your grandmother's grandmother whispered
Soon, dear, it will be over

Contents

Introduction

Rememberings

When I tell the story of my introduction to prison abolition, I begin with reading Oscar Wilde's "The Ballad of Reading Gaol" (2018). Growing up, I always saw the thick covers of Wilde's collected works high up on the bookcase, and thus I understood the book as a symbol of adult reading and of the mysteries of adulthood. When I was around thirteen, we went to Trinidad to celebrate my grandmother's ninetieth birthday. Stuck in the family home, I found my aunt's copy of Frank Harris's biography of Oscar Wilde. Recognizing Wilde's name, and very conscious of reading something importantly mature, encountering Harris's excerpting of Wilde's "Ballad" had a particularly moving effect on me. I immediately memorized many of the verses, and when we returned home, I took my parents' book from the shelf and read the entire poem.

I liken the reading of Wilde's poem to a kind of reverse Narnia. Rather than stepping into the fantasy world from which children are ejected upon aging out, reading Wilde was my entrance into understanding what I keenly understood as serious issues. For the first time, I acutely recognized an accounting of injustice. I grew up in a family marked by colonization where, in my own mother's lifetime, Trinidad had become independent. Later, the works of Eric Williams, C.L.R. James, Claudia Cumberbatch Jones, and other Trinidadian writers and thinkers would influence me, but at this age I had only my mother's family stories of oppression and resistance, which I had yet to apply to a more global analysis of power. Similarly, while I had intimations of feminist analysis as a young girl, I had not yet developed a feminist framework and certainly had not yet encountered the works of Black feminist writers. Reading Wilde was an opening into the world of social justice, of clearly seeing a wrong and burning to right it. I often tell people I became an abolitionist at thirteen.

Around that year, we had to write an essay in social studies class, and while most other girls chose issues such as photoshopping in magazines, I decided to write on women in prisons. This was in the nineties. Looking back, I can assume I was influenced by the dialogue sparked by the 1990 report by the Task Force on Federally Sentenced Women, *Creating Choices*; the public discourse around the strip-searching of the women at Kingston's Prison for Women, which would lead to the Arbour Report in 1996; and even the outrage about Karla Homolka and the perception that she was doing unfairly easy time inside women's federal prison. I heard these discussions on CBC Radio, which my mother listened to as she drove us to our various lessons and commitments. I remember going to the Elizabeth Fry Society in Winnipeg, where we lived, and asking them for resources about women and incarceration; I also remember their bafflement, questioning if I had a mother in prison. I also remember reading an article in *Maclean's* magazine, which I found at the library, that discussed mother-and-child options for women in prison, although I cannot trace the exact article now.

I recount this beginning place because contained in this story is the outline of the shape my work has taken in adult life. I do not think it was a coincidence that this awakening was prompted by my geographic location in Trinidad — on my mother's side of the family, a place of home and dislocation, of diaspora and identity, of longing and return. If I did not yet understand my place in the African diaspora, I understood in some way our position of exile — what Rinaldo Walcott terms the Black Canadian condition, "pre-occupied with elsewhere and seldom with here" (2003, 27) — embodied in my grandmother's joyous entry into our bedroom at the crack of dawn on the day of our arrival, singing hymns of praise. At the same time, our inactivity inside the house and the circumscribing of our freedom, which led to exploring the bookshelves in boredom, was tied to narratives of danger that limited our movements and delineated the supposed unsafety of a Black country in relation to the imagined safety of white Canada. I can return to this geographic placement and tie my reading of Wilde to the uncertainty of the hybrid identity of diasporic Africans and the associated search for meaning.

In poetry, with Wilde, I also found the language to express issues of injustice that now animate my own poetry. Even unconsciously, I can trace how Wilde's work has crept its way into mine; for example, I can match the rhythm and form of Wilde's "I know not whether Laws be right / Or whether Laws be wrong / All that we know who lie in gaol

/ Is that the wall is strong" (*Ballad*, V: 1-4) against my "I know a man who stabbed a man inside and got sent off to the SHU / But he says when somebody comes after you, then what else do you do?" I can also connect this immersion in political poetry to the figure of my mother's father, a calypso artist in Trinidad who once sang the lyrics "Class Legislation" and was threatened with sedition by the British government:

> Class legislation is the order of the land.
>   We are ruled with an iron hand.
>   Class legislation is the order of the land.
>   We are ruled with an iron hand.
>   Britain boasts of democracy,
>   Brotherly love and fraternity,
>   But British colonists have been ruled in perpetual misery
>   *Sans humanité*. (Rohlehr 1972, 4)

I am minded of NourbeSe Philip's (2005) description of calypso as a political language:

> Calypso has the potential of bringing us out of that fugue state where we flee the reality of what has been and is still around us. Using the Caribbean demotic, vernacular or nation language, calypsonians have sung our hopes and our dreams, have sent up the stupidities of the colonial masters, and present day politicians; have poked fun at ourselves and bigged us up; reminding us to remember. (10)

The mixed family pride and frustration at my grandfather's legacy — both his creative genius and the limitations placed by a colonial state on his capacity to exercise that genius — made his language a conscious part of my heritage.

My older sister was my introduction to Black literature. In Grade 9, her English class had been assigned a project where they had to collect one hundred poems on a single theme. My sister chose poems by Black writers, and in my habit of secretly trespassing into her room and stealing her books, I first encountered the voices of the Black authors absented from our school curriculum. Living in a white neighbourhood and attending white schools, we found Blackness on the pages: my sister, finding a copy of Angela Davis's *If They Come in the Morning* (1971) on my parents' shelves, photocopied the image of Davis from the cover and pasted it up in her room. My sister, often unknowing, was my first guide to Black feminist writing and thought.

I can also trace in my child self the roots of activist engagement that cannot be separated from my creative work, scholarship, or indeed from my life as a Black woman. The self that went to the Elizabeth Fry offices for more information on women's housing conditions is found now in the shared struggle for freedom and justice with those behind walls. As Fred Moten (2003) reminds us, thinking and writing within the Black post-modernist frame requires that we think and imagine otherwise. This means turning my gaze toward Black feminism as a method of seeing and being in the world that requires we engage in the canon from a place of lived pedagogy and praxis. As a researcher, scholar, poet, and activist, and as a Black woman, my life and therefore my work is inter-disciplinary in nature. It requires border crossings, rememberings and recallings that begin and are informed by voices from the margins, or as described within Black feminist research, research and knowledge that come from the peripheries.

Living Abolitionist Intimacy

This book is indebted to the courage, generosity, and teachings of many incarcerated people. Some are named in these pages; some contributions are not visible but are no less valuable.

The field of prison and abolitionist studies in Canada, while growing, is still often reliant upon analyses, data, and theorizing by US-based academics, activists, and writers. Importantly, Joy James (2020) critiques the academic trajectory of abolitionist studies, which has increasing-ly located the project of abolition within institutions and away from grassroots organizing including victims of state violence. It's crucial to note that this work did not begin with the intention of presenting it as a book; rather, it has its roots in the urgency surrounding prison justice and the testimony and advocacy of prisoners who continue to speak about their experiences, challenge decisions in court, strike, organize, and resist. At the heart of the exploration of intimacy throughout this work is the ongoing, loving sharing of our lives and experiences between those inside and me on the outside. I name this method *abolitionist intimacies*. Intimacy is both my subject and my research method. I engage ideas of intimacy and their practices through their relationship to state violence at carceral sites including prisons, policing, borders, as well as through purported care institutions such as hospitals and social work. State policing of intimacy through mechanisms such as the prison visit, strip search, and community access to prison is contrasted to the building of intimacy through relationships and organizing with people inside.

The structure of this book attempts to honour this process of living intimacy by refusing the idea that the "real" work only exists in theoretical writing or university spaces. The multiple genres of this book capture the context of what it is to do abolitionist work on a daily basis and what it means to build abolitionist praxis. I do not believe abolitionist work can be ethically done as a "research agenda," and neither does our witness-bearing or commitment to each other end when the computer is shut down and the essay has concluded. To try to speak the prison is to try to bring into words the unspeakable, that which has been deliberately rendered hidden and impenetrable to us on the outside. In my creative work, in poetry, I have tried over the years to speak *with* those inside, to share with their permission their stories and living conditions but also to try to do justice to the words of incarcerated people — to bring into poetry the resilience, courage, and generosity of those inside who share their worst moments in the hopes it might one day help someone else.

To live as an abolitionist, to live in the world we want to build requires us to live differently (to echo Mariame Kaba), to change literally everything, including challenging our own thinking and even our language itself (Kaba 2021).

Abolition is a collective act, and so my book is intertwined with community in the long struggle for freedom that we continue to fight every day and that has continued even as this book was being written. I explore the personal and communal commitments that work toward building an abolitionist ethic based in a principled commitment to collective care. These modes of thinking emerge from a long history of Black feminist theorizing (Brand 1990; Crenshaw 1989; Collins 2000; hooks 2000; Lorde 1984). I use a theoretical lens of prison studies, autoethnography, decolonial studies, Black feminism, and Indigenous knowledges as well as activist praxis informed by my location in African Nova Scotia.

The sections of the work, in creative conversation with each other, anchor the scholarly work of prison studies not only in the university but in a rich tradition of collective resistance, speaking back, and refusal lived and felt from the words of hip hop artists, to murals for victims of police shootings, to marches and vigils, to community gardens that reclaim former prison space from developers (as in the former site of the Prison for Women in Kingston), and in the relationships built and shared as we struggle together in all of these spaces. Taken together, the sections of this work also recognize that the fight against prisons is also a fight against militarization, houselessness and poverty, gendered expectations and patriarchy, and all forms of confinement and control.

In this way, the form of this work tries to capture what it is to live in freedom alongside those without and what is asked of us as we try to turn those keys and break down those walls forever.

Notes on Prison

On knowledge

Sometimes I'll be talking to D. and I'll say something, and he'll say, You're bang on. Sometimes I say something, and he says, Where did you get that? A textbook?

On mothers

My mother was telling me to forgive myself because she thinks that I feel like I'm a bad person just because I've let her down and my brothers and sisters. Yeah, yeah, I play the blame game for sure. But I've learned to forgive myself.
— B.

I drive D.'s mother to visit him. It's a four-and-a-half-hour drive. She hasn't seen him in over three years. Last time she visited, she hit on the scanner. She offered to let them strip-search her so she could go in to see her son, but they refused. She was banned from visiting for over a year. She tried to appeal the ruling, but the prison gets to decide. She tells me this driving up to the prison. When we get there, she starts shaking she is so nervous. People tell me the scanner hits for gasoline, for hand sanitizer, for road salt. We are warned not to use the sanitizer in the bathroom at the McDonald's in the nearest town. D.'s mother shakes the whole time we go through the detector, then the scanner, then the dog. When we get inside, D. comes in and they let him into the room with two remote controls in his pocket even though they searched him before he came in. We all break up laughing.

At A.'s sentencing, the crown reads a report from the psychiatrist he saw when he was a teenager. She asked for the report when he got in trouble as a youth, trying to get him help. Now they use it in court to suggest he doesn't have a good relationship with his mother, that she lied when she said they were close. They use her love for her son and her desperation against them both.

S. tells me his mother gave him up for adoption because his dad was Black. She kept his siblings. He used to see her on the street and beg her to let him come home but she never let him. S. says when he was in foster homes, he used to act bad so they'd have to send him home. He says he can't stand to be alone now; he always needs people around. He thinks that's why he gets into trouble.

There's a poster in the visiting area. It's a picture of a baby in a diaper and pills. The message is that using your baby to smuggle drugs into the prison is child abuse.

L.'s mother loses her job because the police charge her with being an accessory. She ran outside to break up the fight and he ran away. There's a warrant out for him country wide, and he's in hiding. She says the police watch her all day and night. They charge her to try to make him give himself up. Private owners buy the housing she lives in and her rent goes from $200 to over $900. Her youngest son tells his elementary school teacher he wants to kill himself. Then her nephew gets arrested too. I come to see her and find her collapsed on the steps and drive her to the hospital. She needs lawyers for everyone, including herself.

T. is his mother's youngest. When he gets high, he steals from her. She doesn't know what to do to deal with his addiction. Sometimes she tries to lock him in the house, gives him whiskey to take the edge down. When he's high, he steals cars. He goes to his father's house and threatens him. T.'s mother promises to testify about his father's abuse in court. Sometimes she won't take his calls, but in the end she always does. T. always tells me he's doing good, he's okay, but he gets on the phone with his mother and cries. One time he drinks hand sanitizer and falls down and hits his head.

When A. is in reception, he bunks with a guy charged with rape. The guy tells A. he's guilty, but he can't tell his mother. He's scared she would kill herself. So, he pretends to her he never did it.

I'm waiting to visit at Burnside and the couple waiting tells me their daughter is allergic to shellfish. Her food in jail got contaminated, and she got rushed to the hospital and nearly died. She was there four days, and they only found out when she got back to the jail and called them.

W.'s mother emails my work. Her son is severely mentally ill, she says. He wrote a letter threatening to kill me. He threatened to kill her and her husband. He is dangerous. She had to press charges. I hope someone got in touch with you and let you know, she writes.

M. is designated a dangerous offender. There's no phone calls the first six weeks of reception, so A. gets M. to tell his mother to text me, let me know he's okay. M. spends half an hour on the phone with me, telling me how to send boxes, what the quicker PO box is, the best way to ship a TV. Mothers do this for their children in prison. They love even the dangerous ones.

On requests

Akon, "Locked Up." Styles P, "Send a Kite." There is a whole catalogue of songs about being in prison. Why do they request so much hip hop people say, but who else is telling these stories or speaking to these experiences. Wait until you have a friend or child or lover in prison, then listen to "Send a Kite."

Some of the requests on July 4: Joey Stylez, "Indian Outlaw." AR-Ab, "Goon Story." Young Buck, "Gun Walk." Kevin Gates, "Hard For." Jadakiss, "What If Remix."

May 9: Lil Wayne, "Burn." 50 Cent, "High All the Time." Quake Matthews, "Picket Fence." Travis Porter, "Lose Your Mind." Chief Keef, "I Don't Like." 2Pac, "Thugz Mansion."

March 14: Lil Wayne and 2 Chainz, "Bounce." 2Pac, "Unstoppable." Lil Durk, "Ain't Did Shit." Rich Homie Quan, "They Don't Know." Lil Boosie, "Like a Man." Kevin Gates, "Wish I Had It."

They wait the week and call asking for songs. Maybe these are the songs echoing in their head all week. Maybe they're spur-of-the-moment requests. Usually, the caller takes requests from the whole range. Songs come with dedications and shout-outs. When you can't ask for anything all week, hearing a song you want makes a difference.

This is how we show our love.

There's a lockdown and some of the guys get out and call the local radio station. We've been locked up for weeks, they say. We don't have showers and they took all our mattresses and blankets. Listeners call in and tell them they don't deserve showers; they deserve to be locked up. Y. calls them back and says, your listeners are all rednecks. Then the captain comes in the background and makes them get off the phone, and they block the number to the station.

Sometimes I listen to the radio in the car — not community radio, commercial radio — and I hear requests from Burnside. I know the names and the dedications. I know the songs.

I hear Lil Wayne is sent to the hole for being caught with an iPod. Lil Boosie gets out and doesn't know what Instagram is. I. says the songs they request are old and tired and we need to play up-to-date songs, just so they aren't frozen in time.

I'm locked up, they won't let me out. No, they won't let me out. I'm locked up, won't let me out.

On students

I used to teach in a program that was all Black people. I love those students so deeply. At Christmas, I write them a poem with all their names, to speak to them about how brave they are, how I see them, how much they've overcome.

Two of my students, R. and N., are arrested and charged with murder. I saw R. the weekend before, he talked to me about swimming in the river. R. wrote me essays about the monetary system and Africans and Christianity.

After I leave that job, I am teaching in a university and there is an adjustment curve. Students come to my office crying because they got a bad grade, or they had a breakup. I remember sheriffs coming to the door, students in court, students in shelters, students with bruises on their faces, students who never sat with their back to the door, students who got out and had panic attacks in malls.

We make contact again over the radio and he asks for articles, sends letters with questions about books. He talks about his search for knowledge, writes about taking university courses.

When I taught in that program, we believed education was the key to unlock futures. And O. went to prison, B. went to prison. And A. was wanted on a warrant and ran for months, and N. talked to me on the radio from jail, and sometimes I feel everyone I taught all inexorably end up at the same point. Sometimes it's hard not to despair — why we do this at all.

But R. writes about keeping his mind positive, about reading and learning. I remember we always said learning is lifelong, even life-sentences long.

We always pictured what we taught them taking them into programs, schools, careers. Lying at night in your bunk, keeping your mind positive, reading everything you can get your hands on — that's not a failure.

R. asks me, do I still have the poem I wrote about them. Can I send it, please.

On connectivity

A.'s mother gets her home phone number blocked for doing a three-way to his father. Then they block her new number because she clicked over to the other line during a call.

Calls from Burnside are $1.20 per minute plus service fees, so $25.00 of calls costs $32.00. From Cape Breton and Pictou, it's $7.00. Most people don't have that kind of money.

People are always asking me to send texts. Most of the texts are, can you put money on his phone. Sometimes girlfriends text me, I missed his call. Once in a while women text, tell him don't ever contact me again.

Prisoners can send mail, but it costs money for envelopes, papers, pens. The pens are designed so people can't make weapons out of them. Everyone complains they don't write properly and run out of ink if you don't hold them upright.

Positive family interaction has been identified by the Correctional Service of Canada (CSC) as one of the prime factors in the successful reintegration of offenders.

"Family is one of the dynamic factors that CSC has identified as contribut-

*ing to a successful reintegration, together with factors like employment, ad-
dictions issues and others," says Reverend Christina Guest at CSC's National
Headquarters in Ottawa.*

*"Family can be an asset," she adds, "both to the smoother serving of a sentence
while incarcerated and to successful reintegration back into our communities."*

On visits

At Burnside you have to get there fifteen minutes before, or they won't
let you in. You put your phone and keys and everything else in a locker.
It's a dollar, but you get it back. Then you go through the metal detector.
You have to show ID but if you've been coming a while and the nice
guards know you, sometimes they'll let you in. It's no-contact visits, so
there's no search. You're only sitting on the other side of glass on the
phone anyway. Don't forget hand sanitizer.

Visits on A.'s range were Tuesdays and Thursdays, 3–4 p.m. The range
he's on now is Tuesdays and Thursdays 1:30–2:30 p.m. You're allowed
up to ten visitors on your list, but you can only change it so many times.
There are a lot of ranges and they have to keep the populations separate,
so visits are short.

At Springhill they're not supposed to let you in earlier than fifteen minutes before visits, but some of the guards let you sit in the visiting area.
Visits are mornings and afternoons every day except Wednesdays, which
are for guys being transferred to the max. The whole day counts as two
visits. You're only allowed four a week at most, and you can only have
one weekend day because those are the busiest. You have to call within
twenty-four hours to book a visit.

You come through the metal detector and then they make you sit in a
row of chairs and they run the wand over you and then the dog comes.
Then you put your stuff in the locker. Sometimes this takes up to for-
ty-five minutes, and that comes off your visiting time. If there's lots of
people in front of you, it can take forever.

You are allowed to bring up to ten dollars for the pop and candy/chip
machine.

You're allowed to hug or a brief kiss at the beginning or end of visits, but that's it. No touching in between. Some guards look the other way, but some will knock on the glass. One time at Springhill, they call a guy by name over the loudspeaker, and everyone knows what's going on. His girl is wearing a skirt and sitting beside him.

Renous only has afternoon visits, but their trailer visits are supposed to be better. At Renous, after you go through the metal detector you go into a separate room for the scanner and if you pass that you go through the doors into another room and wait until the dog is ready, then you stand in a row and the dog sniffs you. Then you go outside through another door and a fence and into the visiting building.

The inmate committee pays for the machines so if they run out or get broken, the institution isn't responsible for fixing them. Sometimes they're empty for weeks.

One time, A. started crying in a visit and I reached out to touch his hand, and the guard gave him a warning.

On religion

I don't come to jail to find God. God always been with me. Some people come to jail to find themselves or find spirituality. If you have to do that in jail, then you're already lost.

You have to be mentally strong to get through this bullshit. You can't come to jail and go to chapel every day to find God. God has to be in your heart.

I'm not a spiritual person. I pray every night. Me and God are all right. Mentally I have to get myself straight because I'm going to get to the street one day, and I don't want to let everything I have to deal with consume me.

I say my prayers every night, I ask for forgiveness. But that's it in terms of spiritual. But I'm okay with God. And as long as I'm okay with that, there's nothing to be upset about.

I guess you just have to know what you're searching for. — D.

On lockdowns

At Burnside, usually after a couple of days of lockdown they let them out on rotation and they have an hour to make calls, shower, take recreation.

Sometimes lockdowns go on a week, or longer. Sometimes there's no showers. One range files a habeas corpus application protesting that they are unjustly locked down, and right before it's supposed to be heard in court, the guards lift the lockdown.

Lockdowns happen for violence, if there's searches, if there's reports of weapons. The prisoners feel they are also used to punish; after all, guards can always say they had reports of something. They're supposed to get showers, but sometimes lockdowns go on for a week or longer and no one gets out for anything.

A. comes down for court in the middle of the big lockdown at Burnside and he can't shower for a week.

At Springhill, when they went on lockdown there were no calls or visits. Sometimes families drive all the way there, and the prison locks down right before visiting hours. One time I show up early and the guard teases me. "Oh, visits have been cancelled?" he says. I whip my head around and he laughs. We miss A.'s birthday for lockdown, and then at Christmas they go on lockdown again and we miss that too. J. tells me they always lock down at Christmas because the guards want overtime pay.

At Renous, you still get visits in a lockdown. They don't cancel those.

In Quebec, even in lockdown they usually get out for calls and showers every day.

A lockdown dawns on you gradually. You realize you expect a call and it hasn't come. There's no worry at first; maybe there wasn't a phone available or basketball went late or they fell asleep. After some time goes by, you start to worry about why the phone isn't ringing. Then you think something happened. You hope it's a lockdown and not someone being sent to segregation or being hurt or something worse.

Reasons for lockdowns that I remember: Live bullets found in the shop. Someone tore the light down and pieces of it are missing. People have sharpened them already. Fights on the range. Guys bounced from the range. Cellphone found during search. Brews, drugs, weapons. Overdose. Suicide.

The women text each other, Are they locked down? If nobody else has heard either, then it's likely.

Guys I talk to in two different facilities are locked down even as I write this.

On ice cubes

D. complains that guys are scratching their asses, then digging in the ice cube tray.

On guards

T. works in V&C at Renous. On the way in she asks how A.'s doing, if he's adjusting well. She gives the young women copies of the dress code, explains what's allowed and what isn't because she doesn't want anybody to get sent back.

J. says sometimes the guards called them nigger.

I'm sitting waiting for visits to start and the male guard asks me why I'm not smiling. I could tell him, why do you think I'd smile when I'm visiting a person in federal detention, but I smile at him instead.

A lot of the guards at the front desk are older men. They like to flirt with the women. It's best to smile, laugh at their jokes, play along. They can kick you out for any reason.

B. says the guards pick on the Muslim guys. He's not supposed to have pork in his meals, and there was one dish he kept getting — then two other Muslim guys came on the range and they told him that dish was pork. He thinks the guards knew that. They feed the other guys pork and one of them throws the tray at the guard and then they get taken away to solitary confinement.

There's a guy who used to be a CO and now he works for a community organization, but J. says, you watched us shit in cages for years. Who wants your help now.

D. is walking through the metal detector and a guard says something to him about a weapon and he says, No, I only fight with these and shows his fist. D. speaks English only and he's in Quebec. An hour later the guards come to his cell and take him to solitary confinement. They smash his TV. He gets charged with threatening a guard. After five days, he gets out. The charges get dropped because they agree it's a miscommunication. He apologizes to the guard anyway. He has to put in for a new TV.

On laughter

D. likes making me laugh during phone calls. The second time I talk to him he tells me a story about going to court because he beat up a white supremacist. He describes towering in the dock over the two sheriffs while the judge described all the guy's injuries. He tells me the judge is listing everything he did and then at the end he says, "And you had him down on the floor and you went back and so-called 'bitch-slapped' him." The sheriffs break up laughing.

I give a talk about prisons and I tell some stories about D. and it makes me laugh. Afterward someone tells me two "white anarchists" were at the bus stop, and they were outraged that I "laughed at a prisoner."

D. says once, I almost forgot what laughter sounds like.

On superheroes

B. tells me he's drawing a comic. It's about Black people on a prison planet. They have superpowers, and people are trying to steal their melanin. He says parts of it are based on his life. We talk about melanin and the sun and how the beast puts his chemical frequency into food to cut us off from the universe and nature. As above, so below. What do they do when we get into prison. Give us processed food. Mess with our wavelengths.

A. says, is that why you're always telling me to go outside.

On choice

Lw.'s girlfriend gets pregnant when he's inside. He tells people he's going to be a father. But he's been in and out of jail his whole life and she says she can't deal with that, not with a kid in the picture he won't take care of. She makes the appointment.

On dress codes

For women: no tank tops, no skirts above the knee, no see-through clothing. No cut-off shorts. No layers. Nothing that shows your shape. No tight clothing. No leggings. No hoodies. No shirts with pockets. Shirts must have sleeves. No open-toe shoes. No perfume. There's rapists in here, a guard tells me. It's for your own safety. Out in the world you'd say, what a woman wears doesn't cause rape, but I just smile and nod.

On collectivity

A. tells me he's trying to start a poetry collective. He sends kites to other ranges, to guys he knows who write. He tells me he pictures everyone on the different ranges writing together, challenging each other. He wants to call it poetry in motion.

The women always have the most shout-outs. They call out to men on other ranges, all the men in their lives doing time in the same jail. They shout out each other. They are courageous in their complaints. There's a woman alone on a range and it's not right, they say. S. tells us, she's in East 1 right now all by herself and I don't think the guards are playing right with her right now. They're making her time really hard right now. She's struggling as it is, and they're like, they come in and they just gang up on her, it's not right.

Most of the visitors to prison are women. They offer loonies for the lockers, hand sanitizer for the phones for the closed visits in provincial jails, rides back home. Everyone is in the same boat here. Women share information about lawyers, complaints about the jail, wish each other well. It's terrible for everyone.

S. works in the kitchen and makes the call for the other women. She complains, somebody shit on a lunch tray and she had to clean it up. She got out on her birthday, wrote a poem about it.

After she leaves, we can't speak with the women anymore, so we shout them out too, remind them we love them.

The GP (general population) guys complain that the guys in PC (protected custody) always call, so they don't want to. If you see a PC guy, you're supposed to get him. One time I'm in the visiting room, and out of nowhere a guy jumps another guy. A chair is thrown, but we don't have to leave the visit. The idea is, guys in PC are all rats or sex offenders. When A. goes to reception, they tell him he can go to GP if he wants, but he hears another guy had to take a beating when he switched, so he doesn't want to.

On Prisoners' Justice Day, everyone fasts and stops work out of solidarity.

On games

One pack of playing cards in the visiting room are hep C cards. They're black with a Grim Reaper on the back. The cards have pictures of the ways you can get hep C, a needle dripping blood, a tattoo. They give facts about transmission and the rates of infection in prison. We decide to play with the other pack of cards.

Don't get into debt, we say. It's not like Burnside up there, people don't play around.

In Cowansville, they play for cases of pop. Some prisons are lenient on gambling; sometimes they crack down. If you keep a sheet of who owes you in your cell, keep it in code. Sometimes people are getting out or transferring and they sell their sheet to a guy, then he goes around and tries to collect.

I ask D. about why Black and Indigenous people end up in prison and he tells me about the background of some guys from the reserve. Their uncles used to play take a shot, get a shot with them. You have to drink or you get punched in the stomach, hard. He says, some of these guys, they were like seven.

I still don't understand the rules for Ludo. There's tokens and you have to race them around the board. The game is different depending on where you are. Out east the tokens represent armies. They divide the board into neighbourhoods, the Square, Mulgrave Park, North Preston. If you can run up on someone's part of the board, they call that a home invasion. D. tells me about his soldiers. Before he stopped getting in trouble, he once said, I'm a general. I've run armies out of this place. He wasn't talking about board games.

Allowed: 1 – Game system – Game Boy, PlayStation 1, Nintendo or any other game computer (console or hand-held) that does not have data or other communication capability and is available commercially on the market.

10 – Video game cartridges/discs (in accordance with Commissioner's Directive 764)

On love

K. takes the stabbing charges for S. Bb. carries in drugs for her man. She'd like a job at the shipyards, but she has a record now. J. gets six months carrying drugs in. N. did a robbery with her man. B. takes three years for her man and when I visit, she asks how much time he got. I heard five but she thinks it's eight. I think Z. is in because of her man, too.

The number for the radio show gets cut off when the women do shout outs to their men on the other side and a co hears them. Some of them have no-contact orders, so that's third-party contact.

On violence

D. calls me when I am crying, and I tell him I didn't get the job I really wanted. I tell him the head came into my office to let me know.

Want me to staple his eyes shut? he says. Fuck them anyway, you're awesome.

On bracelets

Everyone in Burnside hates the bracelets they have to wear for identification. People keep complaining to me about them. If you get caught not wearing yours, you can get a three-day level. It catches on your shirt all the time, they say. You scratch yourself in the shower. It's not fair, two other guys weren't wearing their bracelets either but only I got punished. Some of the guards say, we don't care but the captain's watching. A. gets down from the max and he complains about the bracelet too. It makes people feel confined, kind of like wearing chains.

On toilets

A. tells me his toilet overflowed and he had to clean it up with his bare hands.

W. tells me down in seg they've figured out how to fish through the toilet system so people can send pills to each other.

D. is the cleaner in seg but there's a guy there who hates him. When the guy is getting out, D. has to go clean his cell and it turns out the guy has been saving his shit in the toilet for a week and he stuffed it full of toilet paper so it would hopefully explode in D.'s face. D's fifteen years in though, so he doesn't fall for that; he knows it's coming.

When there's protests in seg, people flood the range by blocking up their toilets. It gets so bad at Burnside the nurses won't come on the range to give out medication. Then they pay a couple of guys with chocolate bars to clean it up, no hazard suits or anything, just gloves.

On sisters

W. tells me the cell he's in right now in seg is barricaded in. There's steel plates over the slot. He tells me, Ashley Smith's brother used to be in this cell and when he found out they killed his sister, he went crazy, he just wanted to get them.

On reading

R. writes that he has been successful in getting some books for the library. Fanon. Tim Wise. He sends me an article, "On Racism," which he has been reading. I gave it to a guard, he tells me. I write back, what did he say? He tells me the guard was telling new guys not to come on the "Black range." He details his conversation explaining white privilege to the guard. After a few days the guard reads the material and admits that perspective is important.

Two years ago, everyone was reading *Black Scarface*. I tell J. that, and he shakes his head, says people were reading it four years ago too. J. is mad they can't get copies of Malcolm X and there's no programs for Black guys, but they can read a book about a Black gangster. It isn't right, he says.

W. complains that the only books in the library are Harlequin romances. He's reading James Patterson books. After he finishes those, he starts on the Harlequins. They're pretty good, he admits. I'm studying them to see what turns women on.

Q. is also reading James Patterson. He lists to me all the books and series he has read. I ask him if he's worried that he'll start a series and then not be able to get the next book. I've transferred all around this province to read these books, he tells me. When I find out there's two in another jail, I find a way to get there.

J. tells me when guys come down from federal to trials, they bring books with them, and they usually leave them so everyone else has something to read. I wonder who brought *Black Scarface* with them.

I am told they aren't allowed in the library anymore because W. was having an affair with a guard and they get caught in the library shelves. An affair, they call it.

I send A. *Are Prisons Obsolete?* and after that they tell me I can't send any more paper because it's a fire hazard. A. tells me he reads a bit of the book aloud each night to his cellmate and they talk about it.

Everyone is reading Huey P. Newton's autobiography. A. brought it down with him after his appeal. B. tells me about reading the part where Huey is in solitary confinement. He's trying to do like Huey does. He tells me about Huey in a 6x4 cell, with a hole in the ground for a toilet. His way of staying sane was to live in his mind. He lived his memories, B. tells me. It was like living in a movie.

My brain is always just flying. I think you have to learn to control it. That's just my goal right now. I'm trying, when I'm in my cell and my brain just goes everywhere, I'm trying to control it. — B.

On history

The first time I talk to E. on the phone, he says his name and I exclaim, without thinking, the runaway slave! He says, what? And I say, my friend wrote a poem about you when you escaped. I quote what I remember, *But when he busted his chains and jumped out the sheriff van, the nigger in me was like, RUN!* He starts laughing.

On beds

My apartment becomes unlivable. I sleep in my car, on the floor of my office, on the couches of friends. During the day in the office, I nod off at the computer. On the phone with a prisoner, I apologize. I'm so tired, I say. He is silent for a moment. I feel terrible, he says. Here I am sleeping in a bed and you're living in a car.

My friend is out of prison, working out west in the oil fields. He writes about the long days, the weeks away from home. For four years I slept in a bed that wasn't my own, he writes. None of this is anything compared to that.

The women call into the radio and complain. It's so overcrowded in the jail, women have been moved into solitary confinement because there's no space. Women are sleeping without mattresses.

The guards search D's cell. They take his extra mattresses and blankets. When a guard's back is turned, another guard nudges him. I put your mattress back when he wasn't looking, he says.

I ask C. about prison labour. J. tells me he worked in the CORCAN shops. What did you make, I ask, do you know who it was for? He tells me they made furniture, cabinets and desks for the military. D. tells me the last prison he was at, they made mattresses. Who for? I ask. For the other prisons, he says. E. later tells me the women sew blankets.

What's up, S. asks me, and I say nothing, just lying on the floor. Why don't you get in the bed? he says. I say, I don't have a bed right now. He laughs. You're on mattress protocol, he says.

On religion

D. has been in the hole for a couple of months and one day he's so frustrated he smashes things in his cell, and then he tells me he hears someone knocking on his slot. And he thinks, what now. The guy knocking is a general in the IS. He just holds his hand out and in it there's a crucifix, not plastic, real stones, black and jade. And he gives it to D., and he says, here, I wanted you to have it. You just seem like you need it. Take it. I haven't taken it off since, says D.

I'm touched by this story.

I washed it first though, D. adds. You don't know where men's hands have been.

On phone calls

Dn. wants Br. to bring him money, but she has to pay for testing for her child because they think she might have a learning disability and she's already washing her underwear out in the tub to save money. She brings him what she has but it's not enough, and on the way home he keeps calling her and screaming at her in the car.

Rn. calls his wife from prison all the time, threatening her, telling her he'll kill her when he gets out. When he's shot by the police, she says, he's at peace finally; she thinks he wanted them to kill him.

On health

To me health is everything. Health needs to be treated with cautious care and awareness, for it is very fragile and sensitive, whether it be mental, physical, or spiritual. Health is your baby in a carriage that you are forever tending to. — R.

Health is everything, especially in jail. If you don't take care of your health and take care of yourself, for one ain't nobody else going to do it. For two, if you want to be healthy enough to see your release date. Just overall, man, you need to be healthy, physically, mentally, spiritually.

My whole philosophy is, if you're in jail you have the resources to be healthy. On the streets you have more temptations — you're not worried about training, you're not worried about getting your proper sleep, that's where your health declines; it really has nothing to do with stress. But in jail you don't have access to alcohol, to drug, to women, so you can get healthy. — D.

Honestly, I felt I was healthier in prison. You don't have the same stress factors. For me having no children made it easier but everything is provided so it's not the same hustle and bustle of everyday life with all the other factors you have when free. Expectations are different, and you're already at the lowest so there's nobody to disappoint. Only places to go are up or stay where you are. — J.

On geography

D. has been in the hole eight months. He's supposed to have his medium, but his forms come back negative for institutional adjustment and they want to ship him out. He wants to go to Warkworth to be closer to his daughter, but they refuse.

Rd.'s dad did life and he knows everything about the disciplinary system, so I call him up and ask about a habeas corpus. They said he gets aggressive at floor hockey and yells at people, I say. They can't use that against him, he tells me.

Don't you know, he'll have to go out west to get parole anyway, he says. Black guys don't get parole out of the east.

There aren't a lot of Black women in Nova. When I went to GVI, the Black women gave me a bookmark with pan-African beads woven in. F. tells me in Nova they won't let her dance at the socials. They said she's too provocative.

On action movies

I'm told that Y. managed to break into the vents from the shower in seg and crawl through the ceiling. Then he dropped down on a guard, stole the walkie-talkie and radioed an emergency call into the prison.

On gender roles

P. meets a woman in the sheriff van. Those women are so solid, he tells me. I wrote her and I asked her what she was in for and she goes, oh, I pistol-whipped a pharmacist for my boyfriend, what are you in for? I was like, cheque fraud.

On pets

N. wants a rabbit. He's being transferred out to Manitoba, but he only has a year left on his sentence anyway. When we're driving up, H. worries about how she's going to visit him. Maybe they can just wait out the year. In the visiting room N. says, I could call him Mr. Whiskers.

G. is being deported in a few days and D. says he's thinking about assaulting someone just so he can stay. He doesn't have any family in the DR, nobody to go back to. He's been here since he was two. D. says he's running around doing something before he leaves, and I hear him wrong and I think he says he's running around with a rabbit. How did he get a rabbit, I ask.

D. is telling me about some guys catching a chipmunk and I think he's going to say somebody is keeping it as a pet, but he tells me they killed it, skinned it, and ate it. Why would you tell me that, I say. I'm sorry, he says. We can pretend they kept it as a pet.

There's a skunk running around in the yard and everyone spends rec time trying to herd it toward the bubble.

On fighting

When I came to prison, D. says, I wanted to die but I didn't know how to do it myself, so I got in fights. I thought someone might put a hole in me and do it for me. Then I found out I was really good with my fists.

On worries

A. tells me, I've become institutionalized. You're supposed to be transferred from the county within thirty days of sentencing and he's scared to go. He says, I found myself thinking, I wish I could spend Christmas in this jail. That's messed up, he says. I should be thinking, I wish I could spend Christmas at home.

After he goes up and we can talk to him again he says he likes it much better, there's a fridge and a toaster and peanut butter and he's feeding the birds now. They come to his window.

On self-help

E. gets his medium and he leaves, then D. gets his cell. E. is a germophobe, D. says, so he's not worried, he knows it will be clean. All he'll have to do is give everything a wipe down.

E. leaves him a shelf full of books. One of them is a book where you teach yourself jiu-jitsu. D. says, this nigga, now I know where he was getting all those corny moves from.

D. says him and E., they're like Pinky and the Brain.

On coping

B. tells me that he and V. got locked up for a minor infraction. Three white guys did it too, but they let them all out and let them have showers and phone calls. B. and V. stay locked up.

I was pretty angry about the situation. But at the end of the day that kind of, like, made me feel like a bigger person. You know what I mean? Like, they got to go out of their way to try to put me down and break me. You know what I mean? Like, you have to make sure that my mentality is like broken or like clouded or something. I don't know what he was trying to do but I felt bigger like I felt like I don't know I felt like I had some type of power in a way, you know? But they were trying to prevent me from seeing that I have that power. But in reality, what they did was reverse the attitude that I felt. — B.

Do you think you're a good person? I ask another time. Do you feel like a good person?

Really, it's like my mom said, I have to look back and find something I love and cherish and hold onto that and make that something positive instead of the negative stuff.

It's crazy. Sometimes you don't even realize that you're, like, using the past to keep you down and back and stuff. It just happens and you don't realize it until you really sit down and think. I've definitely used the past to hold me back and put myself down, stress myself out. I guess I feel like a bad person in that type of way, where I've regretted my actions.

And I know I'm not a bad person, it's just like, one bad moment really brought me down. But I'll bounce back, I'll bounce back. — B.

On last names

Someone texts me, there was a death in the jail, did you know them. I go to look, and I see the last name and it's the same as someone I know.

When people say my heart stopped, it really feels like that. And then I see it's not the same person, and I should feel guilty about feeling relieved.

On sisters

I read a poem at a march for Tanya Brooks on the anniversary of her murder and her brother speaks. Speakers talk about her life too, not just how she died, not just where her body was found. Afterward, we walk to the Friendship Centre and he tells me about his time in prison.

Prisoners and victims are not separate people.

In my poem I write about how Tanya was a poet, just like me. He asks me, did I read her poem in the book they published from the women in prison. I say I've been looking for a copy of *Words Without Walls* forever. When I finally track one down, I look for her poems.

> *May my hands respect the many beautiful things you have made, may my ears be sharp to hear your voice and may I always walk in your beauty.*

On diversity

T.'s sister was gang-raped at a party by Black guys. When he comes to Renous, he's a white supremacist. He has swazis on his neck and shit, D. says. Somehow, they become boys. T.'s in Stony right now and he writes D., thanks for changing me. I had too much hate in my heart.

On religion

D. tells me Kp. shot this guy, and when he was on the ground, he begged him, please, I have three kids, and Kp. said, God will provide.

On teeth

O. tells me about the dentist in prison. He had to wait six months and he wasn't allowed any painkillers and when the dentist did come, he just pulled the tooth. *We are poor people and they just take and take and take from us.* They even took his teeth.

On grass

I keep telling A. to go outside during recreation. You'll get rickets, I say. One day he tells me, after he'd been in a year he finally went into the yard, and he was so happy he bent down to touch the grass and he overheard a guard say, that kid's been in so long, he's happy just to touch grass. He doesn't like going outside anymore.

❦ 1 ❦

Toward a Practice
of Collectivity

It is the summer of 2020, at the height of the protests against police brutality sparked by the killing of George Floyd in Minneapolis
but sustained in Canada in reaction to the killings by police of many
Black and Indigenous people. Coleman Howe, an elder and survivor
of Africville, is driving me around the true borders of his community.
Africville, a community on the shores of the Bedford Basin in Halifax,
founded by Black refugees of the War of 1812, was destroyed by the city
of Halifax in the 1960s (Clairmont and MacGill 1999; Wesley 2019).
Labelling the community a slum, the city sent bulldozers to crush the
homes, raze the church, and dislocate the residents into public housing.
Prior to the destruction and displacement of the community, the city
denied municipal services like water and sewage while siting a dump
within its borders, a practice of locating hazards within Indigenous
and Black communities that scholars identify as environmental racism
(Rutland 2018; McCurdy 2001; Waldron 2018). Ted Rutland (2018)
identifies the entanglement of power, space, and race brought to bear
upon Africville and its residents through the sophisticated violence
of "planning." Urban planning represents itself as modern and expert,
rendering Black bodies marginal and disposable and normatively con-
structing ideas of the human by determining who can be exited from
public space.

Even as narratives of Africville take hold, driven by the activism and
voices of former Africville residents and taken up increasingly in scholarly and artistic work, the meaning of Africville and its histories and
realities are rendered unstable. Reduced to a circumscribed space (until
2016, an off-leash dog park) in the current visual field, Africville reads
as a small space in the vicinity of a reconstructed church. Scattering the
community has also decimated its histories and stories, often held only
in the memories of the elders who lived there. This is why Coleman

Howe is driving me around the much broader borders of the original community, a physical and experiential geographic practice of reasserting, reclaiming, and remembering. Coleman is putting our bodies on the land, tracing the boundaries as a form of pushing back not only against the past erasure of the physical buildings but against the ongoing erosion of Black presence and the weight of state control continuing to be exerted upon its descendants in the criminal justice, child welfare, and education systems and in the ongoing impact of these systems on community health and wholeness (Waldron 2018).

Coleman reminded me of the African principle of *sankofa:* to go forward, we must turn backward to the past. As calls for racial justice and actions against state violence intensified in the city, his return to the lost borders of Africville and the somatic teachings he shared with me were not nostalgia; they were political acts demonstrating there can be no justice without reparation and accounting for the past. As he drove me around the streets, pointing out landmarks, we arrived at the former site of Rockhead Prison.

Where the prison once stood is now the Leeds Street campus of the Nova Scotia Community College, a generic, shiny, modern building of glass. No trace of the historical building remains. Coleman told me how, due to a crisis of affordable housing in his post–World War II childhood, police vans would drive around the streets in the winter picking up frozen bodies of unhoused people and delivering them to the prison. On this hot summer day, it was hard to imagine even their ghosts haunting the site. How easily these places of containment, suffering, and death vanish. While I wrote some of the poems and essays that appear in this book at the Banff Centre for Arts and Creativity — in a national park constructed through prison labour (Waiser 1995) — I had the same experience of finding myself unknowingly undergirded by carceral foundations. "The Prison Is Always with Us," I call one of the essays reflecting on how my own geographies of Nova Scotia and New Brunswick are mapped by prison journeys, the places I drive through and to on my way to this region's various carceral institutions. So, too, the prison exists through time: in the sites where empty prisons still stand, as in Kingston, Ontario; where they become tourist attractions (Piché and Walby 2010) milking their horrors for entertainment, as at Alcatraz; or whether they are removed completely, as was Rockhead Prison.

In an essay read to me over the phone as I waited for my laundry in the basement of the Banff residence, my friend Jerry (J.C. 2019) described Christmas inside prison: "feeling that you are alone and forgotten, a failure to everyone — including yourself — and that your family was enjoying the festivities as though you don't exist. Men go to their cells and close the door to block out the noise and the reminder of what life is at that very moment." Those living inside prison walls describe being buried alive; how do we even begin to memorialize the dead and lost? This is the final violence of the punishment inflicted by carceral systems: we so quickly disappear them from our memory that at the sites where so much horror has taken place, there is often not even a marker. Not a mark. Those displaced from the community to the prison are displaced again in time, removed again, forgotten again, silenced again, erased again. In turn, new sites of violence arise to replace, modify, or simply reclassify the old: Indigenous containment shifted from the residential school to the youth detention centre and the adult prison system, the segregation unit renamed the Structural Intervention Unit, the street check eliminated as the police invest in surveillance technologies, child apprehension rebranded as "care." In the words of poet A.E. Housman (1898), "And yon the gallows used to clank / Fast by the four cross ways…. / They hang us now in Shrewsbury jail" (14–15): death simply modernized and relocated, never ended and always continued in a new form.

To write the prison, and to write into the spaces where state violence occurs more broadly — the shelter, the halfway house, the group home, the child welfare office, the border — is to contend not only with this present violence but also the past and future of that violence. We must remember to remember: both to locate the prison in its histories of colonial and racist violence (Alexander 2012; Davis 2011; Maynard 2017; Monture 2006) and also to honour the resistance and refusal of those who have struggled against this violence. In "Plantation Futures," geographer Katherine McKittrick (2013) details how the plantation reoccurs in the post-slavery context. McKittrick writes, "In agriculture, banking, and mining, in trade and tourism, and across other colonial and post-colonial spaces — the prison, the city, the resort — a plantation logic characteristic of (but not identical to) slavery emerges in the present both ideologically and materially" (4). As McKittrick argues, the plantation continues to underlie and organize anti-Blackness, "emerg[ing] in the present to repeat itself anew" in contemporary expressions and practices of anti-Black violence. Black death is always reincarnated. Thus, as Coleman Howe understood when he insisted that I return to the demarcations of Africville, the 2020 protests against police brutality could not be decoupled from an understanding of the destruction of Africville, and in turn, Africville could not be properly understood without recognizing that spatial proximity of the community to the prison. To enter Africville is to encounter the prison gate both materially and symbolically, as both precursor and future for the dislocation of Black life. Memorializing the lives of those in prison has both a present and a future urgency: to speak of and in and through sites of state violence is to speak back against the state's will toward amnesia and its endless reincarnations of white supremacy and violence masquerading as reforms.

Toward the end of his essay, "Raising Raced and Erased Executions in African-Canadian Literature," George Elliott Clarke summons African Canadian writers to

> banish the disquieting silence around racially biased incarceration and state-sanctioned murder in Canada. We must examine all texts — novels, poems, and plays; religious, journalistic, and legal materials — to begin to determine the lives of our "martyrs" in colonial, modern, and postmodern Canada and to begin to hear their voices speaking back to us. (2012, 90)

In the African tradition of call and response, I answer Clarke's call by adding that these stories dwell beyond the text. To truly engage the realities of BlackLife (in Idil Abdillahi and Rinaldo Walcott's formulation and title of their 2019 book) and death, we must turn also in our work to the living archive: the Black people who face imprisonment, deportation, brutality, surveillance, and policing in all forms in this place we call Canada.

Clarke urges us to "examine," but I suggest we "collect." Michel Foucault in *Discipline and Punish* (1995) identifies the examination as "a normalizing gaze, a surveillance that makes it possible to qualify, to classify and to punish" (184) — an ordering that takes place in the hospital and the school linking the "formation of knowledge" to the "exercise of power" (187). I am not suggesting that Clarke advocates this kind of hierarchical gaze, but what is perhaps a coincidence of wording allows us to consider how we enter into spaces of trauma as writers. How does the writer also become a detached observer under scholarly notions of "objectivity," "lack of bias," or removed expert? Feminist sociologist Dorothy Smith problematizes these abstract, "objective" categories of knowledge removing people from their "everyday" experiences and reflecting dominant perspectives (1987, 1990).

In this word "collect," then, I think not only of the sense of a collection — of the archiving of Black experience and our project of recovering what is lost, erased, and buried — but also in the sense of collective action — of collectivity — the shared work not of forensically extracting stories but of telling them together. I also think of the call to "collect our people," and what it means to take seriously the slogan that "All Black Lives Matter," and no Black lives matter without the lives of those considered disposable or not respectable.

Collection also has another, more disturbing set of meanings. Embedded in it is also the image of the police van collecting unhoused bodies from the street, the collection of samples from those under medicalized state surveillance (drug testing on parole, for example), the centralizing of Indigenous people onto reservations, the RCMP collecting children to be condemned to the residential school. Collection in this meaning reminds us of the ever-presence of state violence. In *Demonic Grounds* (2006), Katherine McKittrick argues that traditional geographies uphold "the profitable erasure and objectification of subaltern subjectivities, stories, and lands" (x). While the white supremacist imagination constructs the production of space as natural and neutral, in fact these are geographies of domination and colonization that normalize the absenting and erasure of Black people. As she tells us, "we make concealment happen" (xii). The idea of collection, in this sense also tied to notions of cleansing (Palmater 2014, 2017) and hiding — the removal of those who are unsightly, disordered, disabled, or ungovernable — reminds us of emptying space of the bodies deemed imprisonable, deportable, or bound for institutionalization. Canada as a settler colonial state is inherently part of this, as containment, removal, and collection processes are tied to Canada's historic and ongoing genocide of Indigenous people.

The Prison Is Always with Us

In early December, while I am in Banff trying to finish this manuscript, Randy calls me and tells me he lost his appeal. I am in one of the most beautiful places on Earth, where it seems like it should be winter forever. Every morning I wake up to snow-covered mountains outside my window. The food in the dining hall is catered. There is a gym with a steam room. We are here to get away from the world, to write.

While I am getting away from the world, Randy is being held from it. And now, another Christmas in the maximum prison, and who knows what after. His voice is dispirited, although I can hear he is trying to be strong. There's a dissenting judge who agrees with Randy's lawyer Trevor McGuigan that the verdict was unreasonable. I tell Randy what Trevor told him. Dissent is good. Don't give up hope. There's still the Supreme Court. He changes the topic, asks me about my plans for Christmas. I try to keep my voice happy, light, as we chat.

This book is for Randy, and for everyone else over the years who has lived crushed by the state. But what good are words when the judges and juries and crowns who lock the prison doors will never read them? Another world is possible, we chant, but on days like this, the probable world, the one we live in, weighs us down.

When I started talking to people in prison, I couldn't handle it. If I missed a phone call, I became anxious, on edge until they called me back. I carried my phone with me everywhere, even into the bathroom. People made fun of me for clutching my phone or got irritated at another interrupted dinner or event where I duck out, always taking the call. If a visit was cancelled due to a lockdown, I would be deeply upset and disappointed. I cried every day. I remember driving to Acadia University, where I was working at the time, just crying in the car. I would allow myself tears until I got to work, and then tell myself to shut them off for the day.

But it doesn't last, this agony. You think you can't adjust to the trauma, the injustice, the despair, but you do, and you learn to push it aside. One of the things I sometimes say I learned from dealing with prison is to take the long view. You have to learn patience, learn to wait. I'm a person who likes to act right away, so it's hard knowing it could be years to see justice, if we do at all.

Learning to push it aside is exactly what makes prisoners feel forgotten, buried alive.

A couple of days before Randy's call, Jerry called me. Jerry has been inside for thirty-two years. A bank robbery went wrong, and he killed a cop. A life sentence is supposed to end at twenty-five years, but every time Jerry gets close to parole, they find a way to bust him and move him back to a higher security institution. One time they said he was running a store, selling some chips or pop. Another time they said he got close to an officer for information. Just small things, but it's enough to hold him in place. He can't get parole from a maximum. When he first gets in touch with me, all he wants is his parole officer to see him. It's been over a year and the guy won't meet with him. He can't get a new officer. He can't transfer to another province, and anyway he has a wife. He can't get down to a lower security level. He's stuck.

Out in the world, when something goes wrong you can make calls. You can ask questions. If people don't respond to you, you can take it further, you can complain. In prison, they can do what they want. It doesn't matter if it's unfair, or against regulations, or even illegal. What is anyone going to say when the prison has you at their mercy? If someone doesn't want to do their job, you have no way to make them. Jerry just has to take it.

Every time I talk to Jerry, he is thoughtful. He speaks about remorse, about accountability, about amends. He is soft-spoken, always asking if it's a bad time, always thanking me before he ends the call. He's been in so long, he's seen everything, knows everything, and he keeps reaching toward the world, even when it doesn't seem like he'll ever be allowed back into it.

Hope, I told Randy, there's still hope. Life is life, we say, no matter what the parole eligibility date is, but there has to be some hope of not dying in prison. Prison preserves you, people sometimes say, as though it freezes you in time, but the truth is people die of old age there all the time. Once someone said to me, one way or another, we all will be released. I keep believing it will be to the outside. Hope is a discipline, Mariame Kaba says. We have to practise it.

I asked Jerry to write a piece for the *Halifax Examiner* about what

Christmas is like in prison, and he calls to read it to me. The mail won't get out quickly, and they've been locked down almost constantly for months, with barely ten minutes out to make calls. I've told Jerry not to worry about trying to type the piece out, I can record him from the phone and transcribe later.

I am sitting in the laundry room when he calls. The clean scent of fabric softener fills the air, the low rumble of the machines in the background as he reads to me about years past, when cells were decorated and choirs of prisoners formed and there were socials with a Santa for the children handing out presents, and prisoners tried to find some joy in the season. Now, the Christmas traditions have gone away. He talks about not even receiving cards anymore, and not sending them either when it takes a whole day of work to save up to buy one. Prisoners are forgotten this season, while celebrations go on without them, while families fill in the missing seat at the table.

I listen to his voice with my eyes closed. My computer is open before me. I am wondering how many essays to include about prisoners, messing around with edits. Jerry's words are a ringing bell, and even if he does finally manage a way out, it will never be to a place like this, where it is taken for granted that this work we do as writers deserves space, time, comfort.

The works of prisoners are all around us. In my first week in Banff, submerged in pages filled with the voices of prisoners and deportees, I find out that Banff National Park was the site of an internment camp for "enemy aliens" during World War I.

In the library, I find the book *Park Prisoners* by Bill Waiser about the prisoners who built Western Canada's national parks. I open the book at random to find the story of George Luka Budak, a Romanian internee who died by suicide on Christmas Eve, carving his stomach open with a razor and then slitting his throat. I read the passages with Jerry's voice layered over, telling me of loneliness at Christmas, of abandonment, of men going quietly to their cells and closing the door.

These were not captured soldiers; the prisoners were mostly Ukrainian immigrants, conscripted to break rocks and dig roads and cut trails. They were marched in chains, at the point of bayonets, abused, starved, freezing. We bundle up for nature walks and hikes up the mountain. It is bitterly cold. Trying to picture what it would have felt like in a camp here is impossible. There is a masseuse on staff, and the artists get discounts.

Some of the men were rounded up for losing their jobs due to growing wartime hysteria. Some refused to register. Some tried to cross the border to the United States. Reports at the time said the government was "benevolent" in their treatment toward the men. At the end of the war, many of those left in the camps were deported. For the rest, wages were withheld.

There were all kinds of these camps in Canada. Not just the Japanese internment camps in World War II or the camps in Canada's national parks in World War I, but during the Depression too. Citadel Hill in Halifax, Todd McCallum tells me, was a camp for unhoused men in the thirties. Conscientious objectors, particularly Mennonites, were another group rounded up and forced to work during World War II. Over and over again, the same stories. Undesirables, foreigners, the displaced, all rounded up and incarcerated on the excuse of security, or necessity, or useful labour, or cleaning up. We build prisons, tear them down, forget the stories and build another prison.

On another page, I read of the prisoners protesting the poor meals, the lack of underwear, being denied winter clothing like coats and boots. For two weeks in late August and early September in 2018, the prisoners in Burnside jail, a local provincial facility, organized a strike. In their letter of demands, they ask for adequate clothing, healthy meals, shoes of the same size, towels for the showers.

In January 1917, the prisoners were forced to construct an elaborate ice palace for the Banff winter carnival, along with a toboggan run. I'd say it was incongruous, this image of a glittering ice pleasure palace against the broken bodies of prisoners, but it's not. Is it any different from the artwork in the lobbies of the courthouses where we sit waiting for verdicts, or the lawyers that call each other "my friend" as though these proceeding were civil? Is it different from the small town whose employment is revived by prisons, or even from when we sit in the visiting rooms drinking pop and eating snacks and playing card games and laughing? Why shouldn't an ice palace have the shadow of a prison on it, just as a prison can hold love and resilience and hope? It's just, the prison won't melt away, not with all our wishing.

In 1931, the government began employing jobless men in Banff. For some, the work camps offered a form of relief from the Depression. But along with unemployed veterans, unhoused transients were conscripted from Calgary. Kept away from the other workers, the officials also assigned them jobs that kept them from the eyes of people in town.

Many of the transients were immigrants. Brought in to work on the railroads, when they lost their jobs they could be charged with vagrancy and deported. If they applied for food, shelter, or clothing, they could be issued a deportation ticket. Is that harsher, though, than Abdilahi Elmi unable to access medical care or any programs, living without any status?

There was Abdoul Abdi, and after Abdoul there was Elmi, and the same thing happens over and over. And a hundred years ago, only kilometres down the road, a prison camp for other immigrants, the same fears about borders and safety and foreign and danger. There is a building here named for the Trans-Atlantic Pipeline, a tribute to the oil money in this place, and I think, cynically, that a hundred years from now that will be all there is, a landscape of prisons named for oil companies.

It would be the least honest stance in the world to pretend these things dent our enjoyment. I might think about how Banff was built by prisoners while I'm eating my unlimited buffet in the Three Ravens Restaurant, but that does not stop me from going back for dessert. I might recognize the incredible privilege I enjoy of writing here is because someone else died, or less starkly, because someone else is working serving food at minimum wage — but beyond having the thought, what else do we do about it? We comfort ourselves with the acknowledgement, oh prisoners, that's so sad, and then we keep on about our day. As D.H. Lawrence said, *We've got to live, no matter how many skies have fallen.*

The truth is, all our pleasures, all our works, are founded on people's suffering, both past and present. And the truth is, we put it out of our minds constantly. Even those I love dearly, locked away, I have thought on their conviction I would not get over the sorrow, but we get over and move along. Sorrow is not something we can hold in front of us; it slips away constantly.

There are times when my internal geography of Canada moves from prison to prison. When I move around the country with voices of prisoners in my ears, when landscape recalls drives out to remote prisons. Just because it never appears on the signs does not mean the prison is not with us.

There is a monument at the foot of Castle Mountain now for the internees, a statue with the word "Why?" written on it. Perhaps one day all prisons, all border camps, all airports where people were deported from, all roads where vans with chained prisoners were transported, perhaps all of those will one day be places people go to ask why, where they brush tears from their eyes, where they think of how brutal, how unfair things were in the past. But even if they were, I'm not naïve enough to think there wouldn't be some new but same injustice, some other prison, some other safety, some other punishment.

Hope, I say, and try to mean it. There's still hope. We'll find another way. Keep your head up. Be safe. Call me back soon. Talk later.

It is three weeks until Christmas.

An Incomplete List of Stops and Surveillance

1. One of the strong memories from my early childhood is waiting for hours in an extremely long line at the visa office. We were going from England to visit my Auntie Marion in Paris, and my mother, a Trinidadian citizen, needed a visa to travel. My father, a British citizen, did not.

I do not know why that memory stuck so strongly in my head — the line must have been extraordinarily long with all the other Black and brown people, former colonial citizens, who had to get permission to travel. That impression from my childhood reminds me that even before I understood or could articulate racism, colonialism, and injustice, I was shaped by these experiences. Why could my dad go to most countries around the world without thinking while my mother had to be approved?

2. Winnipeg. I am in junior high, walking to a friend's house, when a cop stops and questions me. It is summer vacation, and we are young enough still for long, idle, endless days. The interaction isn't hostile, but he wants to know who I am and where I am going. It is only much later, as an adult, that I see the interaction through his eyes, realize he saw a brown kid, maybe Indigenous, walking through a nice, white neighbourhood, so he stopped to check it out.

3. Halifax. Also summer. I like to run at night. I read a study once that said our eyes perceive distances differently in the dark, so we feel like we are moving faster. At night, I feel strong and swift. *Night coming tenderly / Black like me*, Langston Hughes wrote. I like to run up the hill, a steep rise from the ocean, a stony beach, the moon over the water.

My partner, a Black man, does not like me to run at night. I live in the South End, and he points to the constant reports of sleep watchers and flashers on the streets by the university. He insists on coming with me, but he's not a runner. Instead, he waits at the bottom of the hill, playing on his phone, while I run up and down.

Too often, I have to run back because the police come. White students like to smoke weed by the water or at the picnic tables at the top by the bridge over the railroad tracks, but the cops aren't there for them. Instead, they stop Reed, question him about what he's doing standing around. I run back, hoping my lighter skin does the trick, the proof of his story that he's only watching for me, just trying to keep me safe.

4. Night, same hill. It's my favourite hill. We drive there after the radio show, before we go home, and Reed sits in the car. A white woman comes out with a flashlight, shines it aggressively at the sign saying the beach closes at 10:00 p.m. We are not parked by the beach.

I'm running back to the car, and I stand there and just look at her. I get in the car, and we drive away. I wonder if she listens to CBC, hears me on it sometimes, welcomes my voice into her house when I'm not a brown figure lurking outside her door.

In the car, to Reed, I say, Lady, streets don't close.

5. Dalhousie University. I have marking to finish, and I left the papers in my office. The building is changing the access system, so new faculty are told we won't be issued access cards since they'll be expiring soon anyway. Instead, if we need to be in the building after hours, we can just show our ID to security and they'll let us in.

When I go to security, he refuses to believe I'm faculty. I show him my key and ID. They don't want you up there, he tells me. I say I'm pretty sure my department head does want me to finish my marking. He keeps repeating, if they wanted you up there, they'd have given you a card. He won't let me in.

Black faculty all have stories of working in their offices and having security ask them to identify themselves, as if they broke into the building and paused a minute while stealing to turn on the computer, type some words, read a book.

6. I'm travelling by bus from Winnipeg to Minneapolis to watch a gymnastics competition with friends. At the border, the guards pull me and the Indigenous guy off the bus. He's been telling me about how he was adopted by a white family in Florida, but he's trying to reconnect with his family in Winnipeg.

The border guard searches my bag. I have some books in there about critical race theory. He eyes them skeptically, questions me about them. I am acutely aware of all the stories about how people reading political books can be labelled terrorists. I quickly explain I'm a graduate student. Prove it, he tells me. I'm on vacation, I'm not carrying my student ID card with me. I scramble to think how, other than the fact I travel with books of theory, I can prove I'm a student. I can give you my student ID and password, I offer. You can log into the university system. Why would I do that, he counters. I'm trying not to be argumentative, but I can't help but notice the computer's right there, and how else am I supposed to support my identity. Start quoting medieval poetry?

Eventually, after about an hour, he lets me back on the bus. The white passengers glare at me and the Indigenous man for delaying their trip.

This is the same border where, more remote from the checkpoint, African refugees will struggle through chest-deep snow and frigid winter weather to escape the Trump regime. The news will show images of frostbitten hands, all the fingers lost. My sister, a defence lawyer who volunteers to provide services at the border, says when she goes down there she hears stories about how the locals lock their barns to prevent the migrants from coming in to keep warm.

7. I'm coming back from a poetry festival in Trinidad. When I get off the plane in Canada, as I'm collecting my bag, the phone rings. It's prison, so I pick up. I say briefly, I'm just about to go through customs, I can't talk, call me back later.

Taking the call right after landing might have been a bad idea. First, I get questioned in customs. How long was I visiting, where did I stay, what was I doing. I explain I was doing poetry and visiting family. It's not good enough. I get pulled into a search. They x-ray my bags, remove everything, spreading my dirty underwear out. I try to stay calm and pleasant. The officer asks to see my phone. I'm not sure that's legal, but I hand it over. I want to get out of here.

Finally, he lets me through. He tells me just in case I was wondering, they were looking for imported food. I know you can't hide food in the handle of your suitcase. I'm a young woman, travelling alone, returning after a short stay in the Caribbean. They've profiled me; I could be muling drugs.

8. I pick a woman up from jail, and I need to get her on the bus to a rehab centre in Cape Breton. She says she wants to go home first to pick up her clothes. I'm worried if we wait too long, she won't go, so I'm trying to keep the timeline short. Reed is driving. We drop her off, drive to Tims, sit around for a while, come back. She's still not ready. We sit in a church parking lot across from the house. It's obvi-

ous the place she's staying is a drug house, and Reed is antsy waiting outside.

Sure enough, the police pull up, ask for our ID. Reed is silent. I do the talking, explain I'm a volunteer with the Elizabeth Fry Society, I support women in the community, she'll be out any minute. The cops seem kind of sheepish. They explain the pastor of the church called them. It remains unsaid, but it's obvious he saw two Black people in his parking lot. We've just watched a bunch of white people go in and out of the house with no police presence at all.

The police drive away, but our information is still in the system. Reed is livid. When I get stopped next and it says I was sitting outside a drug house, what do you think happens to me then, he rages. If we ever get shot or go missing, I guess it will say we are "known to police," and "frequented high crime and drug areas."

9. You learn how to get through all the security and searches efficiently at the prison. Don't wear jewellery, or take it off before you go in. You learn the dress code and avoid layers, short sleeves, skirts above the knee, hoodies, sweaters with pockets, leggings, perfume, open-toed shoes. However long it takes to get through the search, all that time comes out of visiting hours. If there's a lot of people, they might do it in waves, and you can lose an hour.

Every prison is different. Some, if you get there early, they let you wait inside. As a bonus, then you're first in line. Some make you go back and wait in the car and only come in fifteen minutes before. Some don't let you sit in the parking lot at all, and you have to go wait at Tims. At certain times, the Tims in Springhill is always full of families and young women headed toward the prison.

Also, the advice from visitors is to avoid pumping gas and wearing hand sanitizer so you don't hit on the scanner. Someone tells me an Elder once hit for road salt and she couldn't come in for months. Stay away from any friends who smoke weed in case something gets on your coat, although the scanners aren't great at detecting it anyway. Basically, touch as little as possible on your way up.

Scanners have a huge false positive rate, but it's not like you're going to be quoting studies at the guards when they're charging you with importing contraband. Smile, keep your mouth shut, joke with the guards who like to joke, look happy. Once you get through the metal detector and the scanner, then the clothes check, you either stand in a line or sit in a line of chairs, and the dog comes out to sniff you. If he sits down, you're fucked.

I read a story about how drug-sniffing dogs eventually get addicted and they have to retire them. The dogs are depressed when they're not working so they sometimes pretend with them that they're sniffing people, let them think they're helping out. It's like the dogs are institutionalized, too.

10. I know the Telmate script by heart by now. Telmate is a US-based company that has the contracts on the phones in Nova Scotia prisons. One of the points they sell to contractors is their surveillance capabilities over calls. They actually pay the province for the privilege of running the phone system; their profits come from the predatory fees they charge prisoners for calls.

The script always tells you, "This call is subject to recording and monitoring." At visits in the jail, they have up notices informing you the area is recorded and under surveillance. In federal, where there are touch visits and not phones behind glass, the tables are clear so the guards can see your hands, and they embed recording devices into the metal legs. Still, people forget they're being recorded all the time. It's best not to talk about anything that could be remotely interpreted as any kind of admission of guilt, intent to commit a crime, conspiracy to bring in contraband, or any other threat to security. Like, if you have a cold, don't talk about how you're drugged up right now. Just be paranoid and careful.

11. Every year we protest the Halifax International Security Forum, and depending on the guests, the level of security can be intense. Some years, there's snipers on the roof. The year of Operation Cast Lead, the Israeli defence minister was there, and the Palestinians came out in force. When the protest started, the barricades went up all around us.

One year, while I'm poet laureate of Halifax, I'm at the city's volunteer awards lunch before going to the protest. The mayor has just come from the Forum, and he talks about how the delegates are so amazed they can walk around Halifax without being recognized, without huge security entourages. He jokes about coming outside to people yelling about warmongers. I'm about to go yell at some warmongers, who can walk around freely in the city we live in while we are forced behind steel barriers.

12. Yet again, I don't get the job, and yet again, I'm lying in bed, depressed and crying, when the call goes out. The Grandmothers by the river have been arrested. For three years, they've been protecting the water from Alton Gas, building a Treaty Truckhouse, and sitting in ceremony at the sacred fire. In the morning, people drove out to the Alton Gas protest site, but the police blocked the roads. Women carrying medicine couldn't get through and neither could the media. Now there's a call to meet the Grandmothers — Darlene Gilbert (Thunderbird Swooping Down Woman), Madonna Bernard (Kukuwes Wowkis) and Paula Isaac (Kiju Muin) — at the courthouse.

When I get the call, I get up, wash my face, and we head out. I think of the line in Virginia Woolf's *To the Lighthouse*. Here I am again. Awake.

CANADA IS SO POLITE

Canada is so polite
It's like someone bumps into us in the Tim Hortons line
And we say sorry
We're always saying sorry

Well, I mean, not to the Indigenous Peoples for stealing their land
And Harper only kind of apologized for residential schools crossing
    the fingers on his hand
And not to Angelique who we hanged
And not to everyone we bombed in Afghanistan
And not for the internment of the Japanese
Or for the deaths on the railroad built by the Chinese
And not for breaking the Treaties
Or racist immigration policies
But we're so polite
We always say please

Well, not to our migrant workers or imported nannies
But they should get down on their knees
Because Canada is the promised land
No, there was no slavery
Just the Underground Railroad because Canada is a gravy train
So forget about the ads for runaway slaves in Halifax newspapers
Canada is a safe haven
For lazy immigrants who come here, and we just give you welfare
Earned by hardworking white taxpayers

Because Canada is so white
Just rosy-cheeked white people playing in the snow and ice
Just snowshoeing and canoeing all day and night
And okay, those things were stolen from Indigenous people too
But we invented hockey, right?
Oh wait, it was Black people who invented the slapshot and
    butterfly goaltending?
Well, we hide that all out of sight

And that's why Canada is so quiet
Because everyone in Canada is so nice
And let's not mention the Shelburne race riots
Or cross burnings or Africville
Or 2000 missing and murdered Indigenous women
But there's no genocide

Shhhhhhhhhhhhhhhhhhhhhhhh
It's rude to raise your voice in Canada
So let's just smile
Canadians aren't racist, we're peacekeepers, we're civilized
And Don Cherry's a national icon
But Canadians aren't violent or bigots, that's just hockey fights

Canadians are perky!
No, there's no dirty secrets here
Canada is just quirky
Like we say zed and not zee
But if you talk about racism we'll be like, zzzzzzzzzz,
There's no need for that here

Canada is never abusive
Canada is so inclusive
Canada is so inclusive, and the proof is
we let other people be here

It's like, I just stole your land and now I'm throwing a party, but you
    can stand at the back if you show us ID
It's like, I just put you in the hospital, but here, let me start you an IV
It's like, what are you complaining for, you got six weeks of *The
    Book of Negroes* on TV
It's like, we're going to hoard all the toys, but we might give you one
    if you ask us nicely
We could acknowledge that you have things to offer us but that's
    not likely

It's like, P.K. Subban
We might let you be on the Olympic hockey team
If you just stop being so Black —

I mean, so cocky
It's not about race, it's about character
We just don't want you to embarrass the country
It's just your attitude, we're not saying anything ugly
You should realize you're so lucky

It's not like America here
There's no history of segregation
That's why we put Canadian flags on our backpacks when we
    travel abroad
Because Canada has such a good reputation
Okay, we get to travel, you probably don't
But you just don't know how to teach English to those Asians
Or build houses in Africa
The country of course, not the continent

Canadians are helpful
Because Canada is so tolerant
Which means we know your culture is worse than ours
But we let you do your primitive things because Canada is so
    confident
So confident that we know better than you
Because our way of doing things is just dominant
We even let you wear your hijab —
Unless it's Quebec —
It's just unfortunate your culture makes you so oppressed
It's not about racism, it's just about respect
For our shared values

But we like your little costumes!
They're so colourful!
Because Canada is multicultural
We just wish that all you people of colour could be more punctual
It's just that white culture is more functional
But we just love diversity
And let's forget about how a majority of the country votes
    Conservative
It's just amazing that so many different cultures go to our child's
    nursery

But then we complain when you get an affirmative action bursary
Canada's multicultural as long as you put white people first
We like your food, fun, and fashion but past that, isn't it kind of
    like racism in reverse?
I mean, it's so unfair how Black and Native people get free
    university
We just want to make sure that everybody's worthy

Because Canada has so much courtesy
We speak English and French!
Okay, not perfectly
Okay, most people only know the French words for cereals
But let's not be absurd, this is still an English country
Or haven't you heard?
There's no distinct societies in Canada

And that's why Canada is so bland
Nothing to see here, just miles upon miles of stolen Indigenous
    land
Just fisherman and farmers and maple syrup, because that's
    Canada's brand
Just fields of wheat and outdoor ice rinks in all thy sons
    command
No, there's no guns and violence here, just socialist health care
    plans
And just ignore the environmental damage from the oil sands

Because Canada is so grand
So good at perpetuating this international scam
So sincere at pretending there's no blood on our hands
Because Canada's not like that, Canada's white as a lamb
And those "other" people, they're so angry
But true Canadians just don't understand

∾ 2 ∾

Re-Collection as Memory

In writing about the attempted deportation of Abdoul Abdi to Somalia, I return to an image that haunts me, a "door of no return" (Brand 2001). Abdoul was a child refugee who came to Canada with his sister; they were shuffled between foster homes for years. No one applied for their citizenship, so when Abdoul was released from incarceration as an adult, the federal government wanted to deport him to Somalia, a country he had left when he was six. Abdoul described his situation to me sitting inside a cell in the Central East Correctional Centre in Lindsay, Ontario, the prison where many deportees are detained before removal. On the walls of the cell were etched names and dates; he realized these were the records left by people before him who were deported. Sitting surrounded by those names, he imagined his own name being added to the list. He experienced this as sitting inside his own tomb. For Abdoul, this exercise of naming was tied to memory and forgetting. He asked me if I would remember him when he was gone. He experienced deportation as an abyss, a space he would enter and in which he would be obliterated, no longer able even to be recalled.

I think here of re-collection as memory: to preserve being for Abdoul, we had to intervene in that deportation. Lisa Lowe's work on the "ontology of forgetting" (1996) that characterizes colonial nation-states signals to us the ways in which Canada, too, is always erasing histories of colonialism and racism, beginning with the forgetting of the Indigenous genocide upon which Canada is founded. Deportation, in this sense, is a culmination of the politics of disposability and forgetting, as the person deemed a site of "unsafety" and threat — no matter how long their residence in Canada or their own sense of belonging — can be simply removed and exited beyond the borders. This, as Abdoul's understanding of the names on the cell wall indicates, is also an act of silencing (Spivak 1990) against which those who are threatened can only seek to speak through traces or "hauntings" (Brand 2001). Those who leave their names and dates seek to speak to others who come after and are themselves removed; the memory-keepers are only those who themselves, in turn, pass into forgetting. As Dionne Brand evokes, in what Christina Sharpe (2012, n.p.) describes as a "desire to account for the no/place, power, vulnerability, and the complex materiality of the body raced as Black":

> The door exists as an absence. A thing in fact which we do not know about, a place we do not know. Yet it exists as the ground we walk. Every gesture our bodies make somehow gestures toward this door. What interests me primarily is probing the Door of No Return as consciousness. The door casts a haunting spell on personal and collective consciousness in the Diaspora. Black experience in any modern city or town in the Americas is a haunting. One enters a room and history follows; one enters a room and history precedes. History is already seated in the chair in the empty room when one arrives. Where one stands in a society seems always related to this historical experience. Where one can be observed is relative to that history. All human effort seems to emanate from this door. How do I know this? Only by self-observation, only by looking. Only by feeling. Only by being a part, sitting in the room with history. (Brand 2001, 24–25)

In Sharpe's (2012, n.p.) summation,

> that un/known door is the frame that produces Black bodies as signifiers of enslavement and its (unseeable) excesses; it is the beginning, the ontology, of the Black. It is the ground that positions Black bodies to bear the burden of that signification, and that positions some Black people to know and embrace it.

In the cell described by Abdoul, this knowing of Blackness only occurs at the moment of precarity; to see the name and recognize the condition is also to recognize oneself as the next in line for collection.

To recollect Abdoul is to return to collect him, to refuse to allow his removal and erasure. To picture Abdoul in the cell-as-grave is also to remind ourselves that our praxis of the archive cannot be limited to paper. Our naming and recognition of each other is not a static or merely theoretical act — it is one in which we actively check for each other, a remembering and recording supported by action on behalf of the liberation of each and every one of us. To enter this space with Abdoul is to be reminded of our responsibilities to each other as living and breathing beings, against the carving of a name into a cell and against all the other examinings and recordings and traces of Blackness found in our files and records and reports and surveillances.

In her chapter "Seduction and the Ruses of Power," in *Scenes of Subjection*, Saidiya Hartman (1997) analyzes the ways in which slave law simultaneously denied Black humanity when it came to white culpability for rape and also maintained Black agency and will in finding Black women and men guilty of crime. Hartman writes, "The law's selective recognition of slave humanity nullified the captive's ability to give consent or act as agent and, at the same time, acknowledged the intentionality and agency of the slave but only as it assumed the form of criminality" (80). In Hartman's reading, Black people become visible only at the moments when we can be accused of a crime. This seeming contradiction of BlackLife was also recognized, for example, by Ralph Ellison in titling *Invisible Man*, as he explained in his interview in *The Iowa Review* with Richard Kostelanetz: "The invisibility, there is a joke about that which is tied up with the sociological dictum that Negroes in the United States have a rough time because we have *high* visibility" (1989, 9).

Hartman reminds us of the dangers of the "spectacular character of Black suffering" (3); at a time when videos of Black death headline the news, she asks us to consider if what we are watching induces empathy or if it further reinforces the Black body as grotesque "other," the bodies made to suffer and die in public. She asks,

> How does one give expression to these outrages without exacerbating the indifference to suffering that is the consequence of the benumbing spectacle or contend with the narcissistic identification that obliterates the other or the prurience that too often is the response to such displays? (4)

In Nova Scotia, the Serious Incident Response Team (SiRT) report (Cacchione 2020) into the investigation of the beating by police of

Black mother Santina Rao in a Halifax Walmart on January 16, 2020, serves as an illustration of Hartman's point about how we only enter the frame when we can be framed as criminal.

While Rao's own testimony or description of events is not cited once in the five-page report, her voice appears only when it can be used to indict her. The justification given for the store security agents calling the police is both the tone and volume of Rao's voice in a private conversation:

> The AP [Affected Person] was on her phone for some time while in the toy section. The tone of her conversation quickly alternated between normal and yelling.
>
> APO1 and APO2 [Asset Protection Officers] decided that HSC [Halifax Shopping Centre] security and the police should be called for assistance because they determined the AP would be arrested for shoplifting. Having observed her demeanor while on her phone together with the presence of children, they were concerned about how she would react to being arrested. (Cacchione 2020, 3)

Under the gaze of security and police, Rao's voice, absented where it might defend her, becomes audible not only to justify the force used against her by police but also to collaterally label her an unfit mother (Mullings 2013; Collins 2000). The arrest is for her children's protection, the report suggests, shifting the blame from the police who brutalized her in front of her children — resulting in "concussion, a black eye, and a 'minimally displaced' fracture of her left wrist, likely the result of being taken to the ground when she was arrested" (Cacchione 2020, 4) — to Rao's "demeanor" and voice. Rao's voice in turn signifies her disturbing Blackness to security, police, and even the implicitly white bystanders invoked in the report. As Mullings (2013) reminds us, "We can see how the marker of Blackness is visited upon poor Black mothers, rendering them devalued commodities who are conveniently pathologized as unfit, lazy, dependent on the state, promiscuous, blamed for being poor, and charged with having deviant lifestyles that corrupt their children" (107). Violence, we understand from this, when enacted upon Black bodies is intended not only to control and discipline us but to save us from ourselves. It is violence that becomes motherly. Intimate.

Elsewhere in the report, Rao's reaction when accused of shoplifting is cited as evidence of guilt and as exculpatory for the police: Rao "cursed and shouted at so1 [Subject Officer 1] and the apos about them being racists and only accusing her of theft because she was a black person" (Cacchione 2020, 3). Here, naming racism and resisting it becomes "evidence" of Rao's "unruliness" (to cite Karlene Faith's [2011] phrase), and thus it not only justifies but invites the violence she receives. The documenting of events by bystanders in the report's reading is not due to their horror at police violence, but rather because her "verbal outbursts were loud enough to draw the attention of and be heard by customers some of whom recorded the ap swearing and shouting" (Cacchione 2020, 3). Implied here is that the customers agree with and reinforce the store and state surveillance, and recording the police is not a form of resistance to state violence but rather a way for innocent citizens disrupted by Blackness to aid in the authority's repression and control. Here, the "spectacle" of violence against a Black woman is repurposed and not permitted to potentially provoke empathy or horror for the beaten Black body; instead, it serves only as evidence in favour of the police, in what Judith Butler (1993) identifies as the "racist episteme" where the "seeing" (16) of white people, imagined as objectively assessing reality, is instead constantly being interpreted through a lens of racism.

Against this report's recounting stands Santina Rao's own story. Writing in the *Halifax Examiner* in June 2020, Rao declares:

> I have been berated my whole life, because of my ethnicity *and* my size. People view me as a fat Black woman first and foremost, so since "she's loud and uses her voice," it's ammunition for them to publicly humiliate me for voicing my opinions or feelings.... Yes, *I am* a fat Black woman. But, I am also compassionate, loving, giving, thoughtful, emotional, radiant, caring, intuitive, intelligent, and *worthy*. (Rao 2020, n.p.)

Rao's defiant accounting of her own arrest serves not only as a speaking-back to the police, media, and public discourses of misogynoir (Bailey 2021) but is also a kind of pre-speaking to the siRT report, as Rao already understands the anti-Black framing of our narrative and how she is represented within it. Rao's public retaking of her own story serves as a frame for Black feminist interventions into state violence.

In "collecting" the stories of the "raced and erased" (Clarke 2012) then, an ethical horizon emerges beyond the question of recording these experiences. What does it mean to write (about) Black bodies victimized by a violent state? How does one accurately witness, without removing the humanity of the people at the centre of these violations and horrors? What does it mean to write in a way that might return Rao's voice to her without further subjecting her to the public gaze? In our call to engage seriously with state violence in all its forms, we must also consider how, as Foucault (1995) laid out, the "examination" so easily becomes forensic, institutionalized, and violent itself.

Fragments for Abdoul and Fatuma

Versions of this essay were first published in the Halifax Examiner.

February 15, 2018: Emergency request to halt deportation proceedings

I'm in a cab on the way to Abdoul Abdi's hearing, and the driver asks me if I work at the courthouse. Kind of the exact opposite, actually, I say. We start talking. He knows about Abdoul's case, and he offers his support. He tells me about being in the cells there years ago, how it's like a dungeon down there. He says names are carved into the walls, with the date and "life" written beside them.

During one of the first conversations I had with Abdoul after he got out of detention, he talked about being in his cell in Lindsay. All around him on the walls were names and dates. He reeled them off, a bunch of them, from memory. Sitting there, he realized these were people who had gotten deported. But the way he told the story, he read these names and dates like gravestones, like it was the day they died. And sitting there, as though he were buried in his own grave, he imagined that his name would be next on the wall, that he would write it down there and then disappear forever.

Later, he asked me in a conversation if I would remember him if he got deported. He didn't mean it like, would I still have contact with him. He literally meant, would I remember him at all. He experienced this deportation as being sent into a state of oblivion, something beyond death, where he will no longer exist anywhere, not even in memory.

I think of this conversation a lot when I think about writing. Sometimes I think about the books I haven't written, the books I could have written. But then I think about Abdoul surrounded by those words. We are the living archive, I remind myself. Our duty to the living, first.

⤚ ⤙

I've been in court for a few murder trials. I happened to be there for a hearing once the same time Jimmy Melvin Jr. was on trial. When there are big cases like murders, they usually make you put your stuff through the x-ray machine when you come in. But I've never seen security like there is for Abdoul's hearing. Yesterday, three border officers searched everyone at the door of the courtroom, and there were more officers patrolling the halls.

This wasn't a criminal hearing: Abdoul has served his time. If you ever thought the border was something benign, the security apparatus brought out and enforced on those of us just attending the hearing is a reminder of how the state polices borders, of the force brought to bear against people like Abdoul, who isn't even here, yet we must all be searched, surveilled, and treated like potential threats.

None of the "activists" present have ever threatened anyone, committed any acts of violence, or used any force. Yet the message seems to be that we need to be checked for potential danger, at the same time as the government is making a case to deport Abdoul to Somalia, a country they say is so dangerous our own Minister of Citizenship, Immigration, and Refugees Ahmed Hussen fled for his life and claimed refugee status. A country the border agents won't even land in for fear of their own safety.

Canada is a country that held Abdoul for weeks in solitary confinement and argued during the hearing that nothing happening to him constitutes an "irreparable harm." A country that took him into care, bounced him from home to home, subjected him to abuse, and never bothered to secure his most basic rights. All of this is violent, yet we're the ones who have to be watched.

This is the Canada that is telling us constantly how the system is based in "compassion and empathy," as claimed by all the form letters sent by our MPs to people who wrote about Abdoul's case.

⤚⤙   ⤚⤙

They really should have mic'd up the courtroom. Had it been a talk or a rally or a panel, people would have been yelling at the judge, I can't hear you! Speak up!

Abdoul's lawyer Ben Perryman was loud and clear, though. That's Ben for you; he seems like he's so quiet and unassuming, but his words have force and they cut through everything.

⤚⤙   ⤚⤙

Here is the casual cruelty of Canadian bureaucracy. Harsha Walia talks about this, how people in the system will acknowledge that the paperwork didn't get done but throw up their hands and continue to inflict harm on people. The system just keeps grinding on. Even though we all know that Abdoul will lose his residency at the admissibility hearing, since they claim it can never be certain, we're just supposed to let it happen. "We don't know what happened," is what white supremacy always tells us when we protest an act of brutality. Wait for the evidence. Maybe there was something the tape didn't catch. You can't draw any conclusions. This is a version of that. "We don't know what will happen," as if 100 percent of the time these hearings don't have exactly the same results. The system always claims ignorance, always pretends whatever they imagine is real. Desmond calls this "white supremacist improv."

Kim Pate talks about how for many criminalized women, contact with the system begins before birth. Even before they are born, there's files being kept on them. Imagine, Kim says, that all the worst things you have done in your life are written down in the worst possible light. What if every time you meet somebody, before you talk to them or do anything else, you have to show them that file. That's what it's like, she says, for women in prison.

In Ashley Smith's case, her file said she was violent. But in the inquiry, it turned out none of the staff could remember her being violent with them. Kim says they put this down to their special skill in handling her. But because they had read her file, and the file said so, they treated her as though she were violent. You can see the videos online. Ashley strapped down. Ashley taped down. Ashley asking for a tampon and being denied. The only violence she did was to herself.

Sitting in court watching the proceedings in Abdoul Abdi's case, I think about how violence is done by paperwork. Abdoul is a bureaucratic accident. Until Abdoul's case revealed what they call a gap in the system, there was no policy in Nova Scotia covering the obligation to seek citizenship for children in the child welfare system. I was going to write "children in care," but every time I would use that phrase, Abdoul would ask where the care was.

And then there's Fatuma, whose name was written down two different ways by officials when she came to the country so every time she tries to get services it takes months to prove her identity. One day, I'm driving Fatuma to get groceries, and she asks me to stop in a pawn shop because her child payments have been held back for months. Just a glitch in the system. This system didn't even buy a gravestone for her dead child, but they have months on end to spend questioning her.

An example of this kind of faceless cruelty: the lawyer suggested that Abdoul losing his job due to these immigration proceedings isn't an "irreparable harm." Once he loses his rights there are lots of things he can do, she said, like appeal, get a refugee work permit, a judicial review of the process. She suggested that pursuing a work permit would probably count in Abdoul's parole conditions as "looking for work." She didn't, of course, say she is going to clothe and feed Abdoul while he waits months for a work permit. Abdoul has a job he loves, a job where he's working to fix the very policy issues that affected him — work the government is neglecting to do — but I suppose if he loses that job and has to, say, clean toilets instead, it's all the same. It feels like what they are also saying is Abdoul has no right to be building more than a bare life — things like purpose, love, or dignity ought to be beyond him.

It's like this system is a monster, and even if you can see how wrong it is, you're not allowed to get out of its jaws. You're just supposed to get eaten, and then do something about it later. It's the inhumanity of it that gets me, how the process itself seems to have more value than any human being caught up in its belly. We have to proceed because these are the proceedings, so they have to go on. It feels like being crushed, like being broken by something you can't even get a hand on.

The violence of the paperwork.

∾ ∾

After, in the hallway, brave Fatuma, who faced down prime ministers and is never shaken, is swarmed by the media. Here she was again, standing strong and tall, speaking once more for her brother. Fatuma has a humanity, a ceaseless resilience and well of love that this system can never match and can never overwhelm. Ben came to join her, kind, compassionate Ben, who stood in the courtrooms against the highest odds and made Abdoul be seen.

I was invited to go to the Black History Month celebration on Monday at the Canadian Museum of History. I didn't go. On social media on Monday, I saw the pictures roll in, the politicians standing on stage, Minister Hussen among them. Trudeau was there speaking about anti-Black racism, words he couldn't find when Fatuma faced him and asked about the deportation of her brother.

I can't imagine myself standing there watching. I can't imagine a situation where I wouldn't have ended up dragged out by security, because

I cannot attend a party on Monday and listen to the government try to deport Abdoul on Thursday.

I saw links posted about how Trudeau "acknowledged anti-Black racism," and in my head I crafted responses, thought about telling them about Abdoul in that cell, about all those names of people disappeared. I thought of writing to them about how when you walk down the street with Abdoul, he gives all his money away to people on the street, how he says he knows what it's like to have nothing or no one. How he talks about the good things he wants to do with his life, the reparation he wants to make.

I raged inside about how Abdoul's case represents Canada's anti-Black racism in all systems — child welfare, youth justice, criminal justice, education, immigration — and I composed a thousand speeches about how you can't say you care about anti-Black racism and see Abdoul as disposable. There is no Black future I care about or that I am fighting for that doesn't have Abdoul and people like him in it. He is not expendable for some other project of recognition.

Standing there — with Fatuma and her child, and with Amina and Masuma, and the people from African Diaspora Association of the Maritimes (ADAM) who have declared Abdoul their child and vowed to stand with him, with Todd and Reed and Brad and the thirty people who came to sit in the courtroom, with Ben, with Idil and Melayna and Desmond and Rania and Sandy and Yusra and so many others in Toronto texting and messaging, who have closed a community of love around Abdoul — I was glad I was standing with them.

We are not nameless or faceless, and our humanity, our solidarity, our belief in each other will sustain us. We are reclaiming compassion — we will not accept it looks like that courtroom. Today, and all days, we will have to believe that is powerful enough, that we will win.

May 29, 2018: Court hearing to grant intervenor status

In court today, arguments were being made in the Abdoul Abdi case about whether the Canadian Civil Liberties Association and Justice for Children and Youth would be granted intervenor status.

Earlier in the day, the city had apologized for allowing "racism to fester unchallenged at Halifax Transit." The city fought for over a decade to challenge these accusations, details being reported in the news as "shocking," culminating in an attempt to run the complainant (a white man married to an African Nova Scotian woman) over with a bus. How is it that city officials, knowing the details of Nazi-themed graffiti, attacks with buses, and threats and abuse would continue to pay lawyers for years to fight tooth and nail to deny the human rights claim? Always endless resources to deny us any justice at all.

In oral arguments today, the lawyers representing the government argued that allowing intervenors is unfair because they would face multiple lawyers "piling on" against them.

If they feel facing two lawyers offering perspectives on human rights is "piling on," imagine how they might feel if they were a child refugee with social workers at the door. Imagine how they might feel if they were a Black youth having the police called on them when they took a car to go looking for their sister moved to another home somewhere in the city.

Imagine being a young Black man facing the full weight of the criminal justice and immigration systems. Imagine actually being powerless when you are taken in, when the education and child welfare and youth justice systems all "pile on" because you are a young Black man caught at all the intersections of state violence and oppression.

Imagine if they knew what it was really like to be powerless.

But to imagine that, you might have to imagine Abdoul as a child. And, as we know, Black people are not allowed to be children. Black boys are viewed by white authorities, on average, as four-and-a-half years older than they actually are and are seen as adults by the time they are thirteen.

If you don't see Black kids as children, and you don't see Black children as innocent, then it is possible to argue the blame for Abdoul not having citizenship is not with the adults representing the state who were trusted with his care but the child himself.

Imagine a government that removes children from their families, locks those children into rooms by force when they speak their own language, sends children into locked group homes when they are overwhelmed by trauma, dispatches the police force to discipline and control these children when they break rules, forces children who grow up in care and experience criminalization into youth jail — imagine the government arguing it can and should do all these things, but it would be unconscionable to "force" citizenship on a child.

Imagine saying you must take a child from his family to protect him, deny him the protection of citizenship, and then saying you can't compel the child to be protected after all.

Imagine pretending Black children don't face state violence every day, but somehow you're looking out for these children and protecting their autonomy and consent by not "forcing" citizenship while leaving them in foster homes where they are abused and traumatized.

Last week, I told a reporter asking about racial profiling that Black people are in an abusive relationship with white society. And here is our government arguing they hurt us because they care for us. It's for our own good. And we deserve it.

⁓

This is what we find in the government's arguments:

Para 43: "The Applicant, suggests he was incapable of understanding 'complex legal regimes such as the *Immigration and Refugee Protection Act* … and the *Citizenship Act*' yet simultaneously suggests that the Province of Nova Scotia should have sought out and imposed the weighty obligations of citizenship upon him despite this apparent lack of understanding of these complex legal regimes. *The Applicant's position is inconsistent and, in any event, does not alleviate his culpability given the application of the general legal principle that ignorance of the law is no defence.*" [*Abdi v. Canada*; my emphasis]

Let's think about that use of the word "culpability." It is not the province that is guilty for not having any policies to address non-citizen children in care. It is not the many adults who never sought citizenship on his behalf, despite being expected to act as "wise and conscientious parents" according to the Children and Family Services Act of Nova Scotia.

It is the Black child who is guilty, guilty even of being a child who could not possibly know the law. Just like Black children are guilty if they play outside with a toy gun and get shot by the police, or guilty if they attend a pool party in a white neighbourhood and get beaten by the police, or guilty if they sit quietly at their desk at school and get tackled by the white security guard.

Abdoul is not allowed innocence, not allowed to be too young to understand (the way white children are too young to understand when they bully Black classmates; the way white school shooters are good boys at heart and too young to be held fully guilty; the way white "boys will be boys" even into their seventies like Donald Trump).

By being a Black child in the system, Abdoul is "culpable" just for being a child. He is culpable just by being born.

And then people wonder why racism at Halifax Transit can fester so long, and how it can take more than a decade for officials to finally admit it, and why the white perpetrator still has a job. How can we be surprised by racism when our own government goes to court to argue Black children are to blame for not having citizenship, and the rights of those children don't matter anyway and should not be heard?

Today the news is talking about Starbucks closing for racial sensitivity training, because white people actually need training to see Black people as human. A reasonable response to white people calling the police on Black people who are just sitting and waiting is, gee, white people just need more of a chance to learn, and a few centuries wasn't enough for that. But a Black child not understanding citizenship law? Guilty.

And imagine what it feels like to sit in court as a Black person and take notes on these arguments, to know our government will fight to its last breath to deny us even a voice to speak about our rights. And then we are told, be grateful you live in Canada, where you have it better than anywhere else. Where racism doesn't exist except in some bad apples. Where we are shocked every time it is revealed, like we were the last one thousand times. Where we wouldn't have to hurt you if you weren't here asking for it by thinking you deserve rights and equality.

By thinking you are human.

June 19, 2018: Federal hearing

Fatuma once told me the reason she and Abdoul do not speak Somali is because when they would speak to each other in their language, the workers would put them on time out and isolate them in their rooms, accusing them of plotting together to escape. It was like being in solitary confinement, Fatuma told me.

I write this as the news is filled, almost hourly it seems, with new outrages to migrant children emerging from the US–Mexico border. Last night, images of "tender age facilities" filled the news, with reports of crying toddlers traumatized by separation from their families.

"How Canada Welcomes Refugees" says a meme circulating on social media, showing border guards hugging children juxtaposed with images of children in cages in the US. In Canada's habitual self-congratulation about what a kinder, more compassionate nation it is, there is no space for images of Fatuma and Abdoul as children, isolated in rooms by child welfare workers. Their tears are an inconvenience to a national narrative that insists, always insists, "it's not like that here."

∽ ∾

The lawyer for the minister opens her arguments by telling us "the theme for today's arguments is the letter P." P is for privilege — citizenship is a right not a privilege. It is for public safety. It is also for policy and parliament, and people, because after all everyone in the system are just people doing their best.

Imagine arguing the rights of children are irrelevant as you try to deport to a danger zone a former child refugee denied his rights by the state, using a format from *Sesame Street* to make your points. A children's show.

∽ ∾

One major way anti-Black racism is maintained in Canada is by simply ignoring the presence of Black people. If there are no Black people here, then it follows that anti-Black racism cannot exist in Canada. As Robyn Maynard traces in her 2017 book, *Policing Black Lives:*

> Ironically, whites-only migration policies were also seen as ways to avoid the racism found south of the border. A major justification for the functional ban on Black migration in the late nineteenth and early twentieth centuries was to avoid the "Negro problem" that existed in the United States. Racism, this suggests, was represented as an American problem that was foreign to Canada. In a similar vein, a historical analysis of media and public opinion at the time found that Canadians were staunchly opposed to Black migration, yet refused to think this racist. It was believed, in fact, that racism could be avoided to the extent that Black people were kept out of the country entirely. (36)

Canada's aversion to keeping race-based statistics similarly functions to maintain the fiction of race not being a problem in Canada. In yesterday's hearing, lawyers for the government rejected research from the social sciences demonstrating that children in care are more vulnerable, that they are highly likely to face "crossover" into the criminal justice system, that they are marginalized in educational attainment and employment, that they face instability, and that the trauma they experience as children and in the system has lifelong effects. These effects, research shows, are compounded for migrant children and racialized children. These studies were rejected by the minister's lawyers in part because they are not "statistics" and therefore not "facts." Racism and marginalization, in their argument, do not exist, and even if they did exist, are not relevant, and either way we shouldn't talk about it.

If you dismiss any evidence of discrimination, then you can also claim it is not possible to know about discrimination even if it is happening.

A feature of white supremacy is that the system simultaneously claims authority to know best but also, at any point, makes claims to innocence. White people know better so they remove children from their family but can't be expected to know enough to apply for citizenship. The border agent has the absolute authority to check a box to deport Abdoul, but also, as the lawyers tell us, the border agent isn't a lawyer and can't be expected to know anything about human rights.

Abdoul is suffering from the neglect to do paperwork, but we are also told the process is infallible, and we must let it proceed. The process "fairly" taking its course now is the same process that can't be held accountable for failing Abdoul. These systems should not be questioned and certainly not accused of bias. To even hold the hearing is "unfair."

It strikes me as very Canadian, this way of doing violence through bureaucracy. One can point to the Indian Act and removal orders for Africville and land titles and all other forms of how the state dispossesses people at the stroke of a pen, but it's also the way the paperwork can be appealed to as a way of disavowing anti-Blackness. The process is colour-blind, after all. We are to think of paperwork as neutral, as something beyond human agency. It's a polite way of killing people, checking the boxes and throwing up your hands and saying the process must prevail.

While the minister's delegate cannot possibly be expected to comprehend human rights in Canada (but yet is qualified to make decisions), Abdoul is "culpable" as a child for not understanding citizenship law and not actively seeking a citizenship lawyer as a minor child in care to advocate for his own citizenship — despite minors being unable until

2017 to apply for citizenship on their own behalf. The only person guilty in this scheme is the Black child.

∾ ∾

When Abdoul didn't even have a lawyer, he submitted that his mother was dead, and his father was missing and he didn't know where he was. Later, he told agents both of his parents were murdered. Now, the government argues that Abdoul's lack of memory or knowledge about his family isn't a sign of trauma but rather evidence of him willfully lying to agents.

Perhaps a child who spent the first six years of his life in refugee camps, who fled to Canada at age six and grew up in care separated from his family, might understandably not know about or remember what happened to his parents. Instead, they again blamed the refugee child for not knowing, all while arguing it's insignificant that adults did not know crucial parts of their job such as the Charter of Rights or the need to obtain citizenship for refugee children.

The minister's delegate also questioned Abdoul's closeness to his family and whether or not he has a relationship with his daughter. I am reminded of how, during enslavement, when Black families were separated it was imagined Black parents felt no more pain than "pups being taken from a bitch."

While denying the existence of anti-Black racism during the hearing, it was the Black refugee child who was imagined as somehow oppressing all these powerful systems. He was the one being "unfair": how terrible of Abdoul to suggest that he was mistreated in the child welfare system or that the immigration system reveals anti-Black bias. Truly, these are the real victims in this case.

During yesterday's hearing I thought about how victims of sexual assault are doubted, how trauma is discounted, how they are framed as liars or unreliable. The courts are increasingly under pressure to not allow questions and arguments that draw upon stereotypes of victims, and there is criticism of defence lawyers who rely upon these stereotypes.

At yesterday's hearing, the trauma of a Black child was dismissed and deemed irrelevant. Black experiences are "unfounded." Abdoul was misleading agents when he said he couldn't remember his family, and his narrative about the abuse he experienced in care was "not supported by the record." The systems that wash their hands of Abdoul now show us those hands and tell us they are clean.

∽ ∾

P is for Perryman. "This is a judicial review application, not an episode of *Sesame Street*," said Ben. "Justice isn't supposed to be like the Snuffleupagus, something that isn't here right now, but exists and might appear at some uncertain point down the road."

July 17, 2018: Ralph Goodale announces Abdoul will not be deported

I get a call from Desmond. When I pick it up, Ben is on the line too. Ralph Goodale just tweeted the government will respect the court's ruling on July 13, and Abdoul will not be deported.

We've been through too much, lived long enough, to get too excited. I wonder if maybe someone hacked into Goodale's account, but who would hack into a minister's Twitter to talk about Abdoul? Nobody has called Ben or Abdoul to tell them the deportation is over. After all these months, his life is saved in a tweet put out at 9:00 p.m., right before a cabinet shuffle.

All those court hearings, all the briefs filed, all the arguments, the news stories, the endless interviews, the questions to Trudeau, the emails written, the phone calls, the thousands of tweets, the money the government spent arguing against his rights, coming down to two sentences: "The Government of Canada respects the decision filed on July 13 by the Federal Court of Canada concerning Abdoul Abdi. The Government will not pursue deportation for Mr. Abdi."

Sitting in Idil's apartment with Abdoul months ago, he heard me give an interview about his case. When I got off the phone, he said, with some wonder, "You're really taking this seriously."

I would burn this all down for you, I tell him, and I mean it. Before we started this, we asked each other: How far are we willing to go? Would we drain our bank accounts? Would we get on a plane? Would we lie down on the runway? And yes, yes, yes, we would do anything. We have to be willing, because our will and our love is the only thing standing between Abdoul and the government, beween Abdoul and the abyss. Our love is what started this, what has held us. We would never have let him go gently.

July 29, 2018

Abdoul comes to see me before a workshop I am giving with Black Lives Matter–Toronto. I am standing on the street waiting for him. When he sees me, he grabs me into a hug, lifts me off my feet. He is free. I am crying. It is the most joy I have ever felt in my life.

THE BORDERS CROSSED US

They sailed around the world until they hit Hispaniola
The Pope and Queen and banks all said, let roll the mighty dollar
Columbus and Cortez they claimed they were explorers
The borders crossed us, we never crossed the borders

Set up the encomienda system for the ones they called the
    Indians
Justified it all because they said their souls weren't Christians
Forced the tribes to work, stole the land acre by acre
Took the people as a tribute, the resources and the labour

The ones they didn't murder they took out with disease
Ninety-five percent of the Americas murdered within the century
The Arawak, Taíno, and Carib they said they were animals
Enslaved and exterminated on the claim they were cannibals

And when few were left to work the land because they were all
    dead
They turned their eyes to Africa and said, enslave the Blacks
    instead

So they sent their ships to prey upon West African shores
Ironically guided by the maps taught them by the Moors
To the Company of Royal Adventurers from the conquistadors
The borders crossed us, we never crossed the borders

They claimed they were too delicate to work out in the heat
They said we didn't feel the pain because we were like beasts
They developed racist ideologies to say we were inferior
And so the colour of our skin became their human criteria

And with letters from the Queen, they bought and then they sold
And stacked upon each other they chained us in the hold
To work the land for sugar they brought us across the sea
Brutalized and murdered, took us from our families

Saw us just like cattle so we could be exported
The average life ten years until we expired from the torture
And millennia of history and humanity they had to ignore
The border crossed us, we never crossed the borders

We worked the fields for them, condemned 'cause we were Black
And in Europe they built cathedrals and museums from the
    wealth got off our backs
The developed world they call it, the cradle of civilization
Funded by the labour of forced African migration

Factories and manufacturing, banks, technology, and ports
The Industrial Revolution from the goods sent back and forth
And corporations and royal charters developed of all sorts
The borders crossed us, we never crossed the borders

Now five hundred years later they call themselves the first-world
    nations
Now they got the nerve to say they're controlling immigration
And them that only ran into the Americas 'cause they was lost
Now say they define our movement and the spaces that we cross

And now brown and Black people from the Global South to North
Have to apply to enter countries where once our movement here
    was forced
Trade in sex and labour is the modern slavery
Taken from the same people exploited through history

One percent of the population own forty percent of the world's
    assets
Globalization should be called the continuation of the Middle
    Passage
From the Hudson's Bay Company to mass extermination
They take the lives from people, give the rights to corporations

Land, jobs, and resources, the people can't afford it
Parents leave their children just so they can support them
From nannies to fruit pickers, they make domestic labour laws
Forcing movement of the people just like they did before

Taking rights over their bodies just because they're poor
Lock workers into rooms, seize papers and passports
Imprisoned, killed at checkpoints, exploited and deported
The borders crossed us, we never crossed the borders

And now from Jamaica, Guatemala, Philippines, and Mexico
The wretched of the earth still make the dollars flow
When half the world's workers labour for a dollar and a quarter
The borders crossed us, we never crossed the borders

Babies born in prison because their mothers are detained
Workers die on highways in vans where they are chained
Women raped and abused but no one can report it
The borders crossed us, we never crossed the borders

Still working in the fields, still caring for the children
No citizenship, health, education, or standard of living
Come here for a season and then they are transported
The borders crossed us, we never crossed the borders

And the same people who through history have colonized the
        rest
Continue to take the land and hoard up all the wealth
Still living off the backs of everyone they slaughtered
The borders crossed us, we never crossed the borders

Still don't want to pay a living wage, workers at their beck and
        call
Our bodies and our freedom, they want to own them all
Say we are illegal, but our history records
The borders crossed us, we never crossed the borders
The borders crossed us, we never crossed the borders

POEM FOR JUDGES

Good morning, judges
I hope you didn't have to spend too long sitting down
Now imagine twenty-three hours a day without moving around
That's what they call segregation
There's people living there right now

Did you open a door today under your own power?
Did anyone watch you while you were taking a shower?
Maybe you're feeling tired and you go to take a stretch
Well, this hand's your toilet, and this hand's your desk
And just to check if you're still alive
Did you put your hand to your chest
Because you're down in the hole without any mental stimulation?

Did you talk to your colleagues today?
Did you have human conversation?
Or did you start to slice up your arm just to feel stimulation
Okay, maybe that's extreme
Let's take it back to population

Did someone hug you when they saw you?
Maybe a kiss on the cheek
Now imagine nothing touching you but handcuffs for week after
    week
Is your back to the wall because you can't have anyone behind?
Did someone string themselves up next to you?
Did you hear them die?
And then shove your emotions down because prison's not the
    place to cry
Unless you wanna look weak

Did you have things so terrible happen to you that you can't even
    speak?
But we call them just doing time
Just what happens when you offend
Did you have a good weekend?
Did you visit with family and friends?

After they left did anyone tell you to take your clothes off and
    bend?

Is your body your own?
Is humiliation just a daily act?
Did you send a text on your phone and get a text back?
Something so simple as human contact

Did you smile today?
Maybe you laughed
Did you smell fresh air or touch a blade of grass?
Now look at the second hand on your watch and think how slow
    time can pass

Did you go to your mother's funeral or your child's first day of
    class?
Did you talk to your children on a phone behind glass?

Smell your clothes
Did you wash and change them all week?
Or maybe you're eighteen on a range, too scared to come out 'til
    everyone's asleep
Were the lights on all night while you lay down in your bed?
Did you smell somebody else's body waste in the toilet at your
    head?

I'm not telling you the horrors
I'm just telling you the day-to-day
And I know you're just a human being, but now strip that
    humanity away
And since you're only human, I'm sure you've made mistakes
But that's the thing about the rest of us, it seems that we get
    breaks
And this poem's a couple of minutes and then you get to walk
    away

But if you're sentenced on a range, well then you have to stay
Until you dream about walking through the walls
And you wake up still inside it all

And there's someone screaming and banging just across the hall
And if you try to take your life, you have to push a button just to
    call
And they'll put you in a gown in a cell and watch you day and
    night
And you won't get any help, so it's better just to lie

And then maybe it starts to feel normal
That's the most frightening thing to know
Because now even if you can get out, you're not sure how it's
    going to go
And you haven't touched a door in so long or just shit when you're
    alone

And your family won't understand when you jump at every sound
And you can't sleep in bed with the one you love
Because you're scared you'll wake up with your hands around
    their neck
And your heart's beating in your chest so hard you have to take
    your hand to check
And maybe you start to think it's easier to go back to a cell
Between a toilet and the desk

What it's like for people doing time in prison, I can't begin to tell
And I know you're human beings who just try to do your duty well
We can read the judgment, but we'll never smell the smell
Or feel ourselves go numb
Or wait for release dates that don't ever seem to come

You can hear this poem, and then you don't have to stay
You can say you're only human
Now strip that humanity away

ℰ 3 ℰ

Erasure and the
Slow Work of Liberation

As is the case for Black Studies generally in Canada, one gap re-vealed in the *Abolition in So-Called Canada Syllabus* (2020) is in abolitionist writing focusing on Black people incarcerated in Canada. First published on Prisoners' Justice Day in 2019 and updated again in 2020, the *Syllabus* is a "living, collectively authored document … Assembled and updated by a group of abolitionist activists, community members, lawyers, and scholars, the syllabus was first created to fill the gaps in classroom and community education regarding prison abolition" (2020, 2). While the works of Angela Davis, Michelle Alexander, Ruth Wilson Gilmore, Mariame Kaba, and other Black feminist abolitionists in the US continue to importantly frame our understandings of Black incarceration and the "afterlife of slavery" (Hartman 2007, 6), Black incarceration in Canada, discourse around it, and Canada's history of anti-Blackness continues to be largely hidden. And, as Clarke (2012) identifies in "Raising Raced and Erased Executions," Black Canadian writing has not often turned to the prison as a site of study.

Anthony Morgan (2018) observes that the persistent Canadian nar-rative of we are "not like that" in comparison to the United States stifles Canadian discussion and recognition of anti-Blackness and the violence visited upon Black people by this state apparatus:

> Too routinely, Black bodies are unjustly surveilled, intercepted, and snuffed out by police in the Great White North. Not only is anti-Black racism real here, but it is forcefully denied when you try to point it out. As such, there exists a double burden of anti-Blackness in Canada. This is what I call the suffocating experience of being Black in Canada. (2018, n.p.)

Sherene Razack (2002) notes that in the settler-colonial imagination, the "Great White North" is imagined as empty and wild until tamed by white "discoverers" to whom the land then rightfully belongs. Indigenous Peoples are erased from the landscape, while all other people become newcomers who should be properly grateful to be welcomed by generous and benevolent whites. Indigenous scholars including Pamela Palmater (2014), Glen Coulthard (2014), Bonita Lawrence (2003), and Leanne Betasamosake Simpson (2017) make clear the genocidal foundations of Canada and Canada's ongoing colonization of Indigenous Peoples and Nations; the criminalizing of Indigenous Peoples is directly tied to the removal of Indigenous Peoples from land, the theft of resources, and the disregard of Indigenous sovereignty in favour of corporations, extractive industries, and state profit from these entities. Abolition must reckon with this originating crime scene: as the slogan says, there can be no justice on stolen land.

As argued by Robin Winks, Katherine McKittrick, Afua Cooper, Rinaldo Walcott, George Elliott Clarke, Dionne Brand, James Walker, Agnes Calliste, M. NourbeSe Philip, and Carl James, among others, Black Canadians are consistently wiped from the Canadian consciousness: histories of enslavement are buried, forgotten, and denied; school curricula exclude and elide Black histories, literatures, and contributions; publishing houses ignore Black writing; and white colonial space is consistently imagined as emptied of Black presence even as markers and names of slavery and colonization litter the landscape (Mugabo 2019). Prisons are living monuments to racism and colonial violence in Canada.

Against these silencings, gaps, and erasures, the task of not only creating abolitionist literature but in living in abolitionist relationship to the world requires understanding the production of abolitionist work, thinking, and literature differently. At any site where Black people speak, there will always be attempts at repression. On the *Black Power Hour* radio show, we work to make the space one in which the voices and needs of incarcerated people are centred. This means providing the programming that the people in jail want, and for the majority of our listeners, this is expressed through hip hop. In the format of the show, we engage in discussion of topics chosen by incarcerated listeners through the week that deal with political, social, cultural, historical, and news topics, with an emphasis on news about prisoner rights, policing, and abuses of state authority as well as stories of resistance to state control. In between the conversation, and for the final half hour of the show, people can request any music they like; often people outside call in to send requests to loved ones inside, and those inside call to request music they would like to hear. Early on in our programming, we understood the importance of requests: when you are incarcerated and have no control over your body, when your most personal acts such as using the toilet are viewed on camera, when you cannot move how and where you want to, the opportunity to make a request and to have it played may be the only time in the week where you can ask for something and have it. Many of the frequently requested songs are those that relate to the conditions of people who are incarcerated, that tell narratives of being in prison, of life on the streets, of violence, of drug use, and so on. As Robin D.G. Kelley identifies, rappers "come close to providing what Michel Foucault calls a 'counter-discourse of prisoners'" (1996, 196). Whether or not we like the songs or enjoy the lyrics is not the issue; what is important is that a space is provided where people can exercise some small agency denied them elsewhere.

Frequently in the show's early days, these music choices were the source of constant complaint and contention. On one occasion, a white woman programmer complained to the station and threatened to complain to the Canadian Radio-television and Telecommunications Commission (CRTC) to have the entire station's licence pulled; the threat of Blackness is so contaminating, the babies must be thrown out with the bathwater. People complained repeatedly about the language in the music, from the use of the n-word in songs, to "profanity," to "glorification" of crime. When we received these complaints, I would respond that the true obscenity is that people who participate in the show can be held in solitary confinement; what is offensive is that carceral institutions force pregnant women to sleep without mattresses, place people in "dry cells" where their bowel movements are monitored and searched, where people on suicide watch are stripped naked, and where basic human rights like sunlight are denied. The issue was not only the language of the songs but specifically the context of Blackness and the perceived audacity of people who are incarcerated daring to listen to music about criminal activity. The imposition of a policing gaze upon music and the music choices of incarcerated people demonstrates how people beyond the prison designate themselves as cops and take on the role of disciplining and controlling those marked by criminalization. It specifically rankles many complainants that "criminals" might listen to music about crime, and we are expected to remove that choice, as if music were responsible for social problems. This is a reading of Blackness as pathology that places responsibility for Black criminalization on Black culture and not on enslavement, deprivation, the constant extortion of resources from our communities, gentrification, educational pushout, and a lack of health care and trauma care.

Like the censorship, policing, and criminalization of hip hop (particularly in the nineties, notoriously including the prosecution of 2 Live Crew [Crenshaw 1997]), the policing of "obscenity" on our radio show is deeply tied to carceral mentalities in the broader community. One email from a white female programmer explicitly tied together her objection to both the music and the prisoners' voices, noting the show should be called "prison profanity hour" and adding that the incarcerated listeners and speakers had nothing to say that should be heard. Her objection was to the song "Riot" by Young Buck (2016), which we played only days after the Philando Castile shooting in 2016. Young Buck urges,

> Let's start a motherfucking riot
> Load it pick it up and fire it
> You wonder why us niggas keep dying.

This white woman objected to the use of the n-word and "motherfucking," asserting as a mother she found the lyrics offensive. That Black mothers lose their children to police violence did not matter to her. That the state fucks Black mothers in all ways also did not occur to her. Preserving her frame of innocent, pure, untouched white motherhood was deemed more important than Black people expressing anger over police killings; in fact, she suggested that her use of a Buddhist quotation on her show in response to the police murder was the appropriate one, as it urged love.

The sounds of criminalized Blackness are considered beyond the speakable, the limits of what should be spoken. For example, Kelley, discussing hip hop in the nineties landscape of "postindustrial" Los Angeles, notes:

Hip hop's challenge to police brutality sometimes moves beyond the discursive arena. Their music and expressive styles have literally become weapons in a battle over the right to occupy public space ... The "noise" constitutes a form of cultural resistance that should not be ignored, especially when we add those resistive lyrics about destroying the state or retaliating against the police. (1996, 195)

In another example, in her essay about the prosecution of 2 Live Crew Kimberlé Crenshaw (1997) applies a Black feminist framework that both recognizes the racism of the prosecution and also addresses the misogyny toward Black women. As she notes, the public outrage about hip hop lyrics professes concern for the representation of Black women, but "Black women appear to function as stand-ins for white women" (258). While refusing to accept the idea that "Black women are expected to be vehicles for notions of 'liberation' that function to preserve Black female subordination" (261), Crenshaw simultaneously asserts, "nothing about the anti–2 Live Crew movement is about Black women's lives ... the racism of that process is injurious to us" (262).

As a Black woman co-creating the radio show, I felt that this apparent outrage at sexist lyrics ignored the work Black women do in community to create collective space. Music offers an entry point from which political discussion can take place. This fraught work of building abolitionist platforms clawed back from carceral control — the jail rapidly blocked the station phone number, and they frequently tune communal TVs to the same frequency as the station to prevent listening — is ignored in favour of white constructions of what is violent, what is offensive, and what should occupy public space and airwaves. This is only one example of the ways in which the abolitionist work taking place in community doesn't make it into text. Our abolitionist syllabi, therefore, must not only encourage and amplify Black public writing about abolition but also recognize other spaces beyond the written text where abolitionist organizing is happening, particularly those created and maintained by Black women — spaces such as the African Nova Scotian church where congregation members welcome incarcerated people to funerals, as I write about with Randy Riley (2020); spaces created by women who faithfully visit prisons across the region with the African United Baptist Association of Nova Scotia; and the abolitionist work of women who pack boxes, attend court, and care and watch out for children while a parent is gone. These women do not have time to write down their abolitionist theory; they are busy doing abolition labour. Our archiving must acknowledge and hold these sites as well.

Echoing Clarke (2012), we must include the records left in habeas complaints that attest to conditions, the letters to the Parole Board on behalf of incarcerated people that testify about their lives, and the cultural reports that speak to the conditions of their lives and the ongoing impacts of anti-Black racism on neighbourhoods and families. In discussing the case of R. v. "X" — the "first 'Cultural Assessment' of an African Canadian youth [that] was presented and tested as evidence in a sentencing hearing in Canada" (Wright 2016, 1), African Nova Scotian social worker Robert S. Wright notes, "given the prevalence of clinical reports offered at sentencing, many of which will make little reference to the racial location of their subject, it is important that writers of Cultural Assessments be sufficiently qualified to contextualize and perhaps even rebut other assessments" (2). Just as Saidiya Hartman (1997) identifies, Blackness appears so that it can be criminalized and is ever-present as a marker of degeneracy; yet, mention of race is absent from any of the official reports or assessments in Canadian sentencing hearings. Wright notes, given a context through which to view the life of "X," an African Nova Scotian youth charged with shooting his cousin and threatened with sentencing as an adult, Judge Anne Derrick was able to shift her seeing. She writes that Wright's evidence "raises significant questions about the assessment of 'X' as a criminally entrenched, sophisticated youth. It provides a more textured, multi-dimensional framework for understanding 'X', his background, and his behaviours"; Derrick adds, it "gives me a lens through which to view 'X'" (Wright 2016, 1). In quoting this report, I locate it as a site in which the slow, compromised, strategic work of liberation takes place, remembering that for Black people abolition cannot always be theoretical but is lived out in all the ways we come up against the system and try only to slip in a Black finger between the lock. We know it does not end the prison, but we also know enslavement has never ended, either. In the "freedom" granted us inside white society, abolition also means doing the best we can for every day less in prison.

In a conversation between Syrus Marcus Ware and Giselle Dias (Niigaanii Zhaawshko Giizhigokwe) published in *Until We Are Free* (2020), Ware argues,

> For me, true abolition would only come through a revolution-
> ary process where everything would change ... Abolition is, yes,
> the closing and ending of our reliance on the prison-industrial
> complex as a way of handling our conflict, but it's also an entire-
> ly new way of being and relating to each other in the world. (33)

Abolition in this philosophy is not just about eliminating material structures of incarceration and punishment such as prisons and police; it is
more deeply about shifting our relationships to land, to capitalism, to
each other, and to ourselves. As Moten and Harney (2013) ask,

> What is, so to speak, the object of abolition? Not so much the
> abolition of prisons but the abolition of a society that could
> have prisons, that could have slavery, that could have the wage,
> and therefore not abolition as the elimination of anything but
> abolition as the founding of a new society. (42)

Abolition is also the shifting of knowledge hierarchies away from the
idea that justice is the province of a few highly trained law experts and
academics. Instead, we know the work of abolition lives in our communities every day, including in our refusal to abandon or dehumanize
those living inside the walls.

Thirteen Ways of Looking at My Blackness

A version of this essay was first published in the Halifax Examiner *on December 17, 2016.*

1. I am four or five years old. We live in a small village in England and my mother's sisters come to visit. I have never seen Black people before. I do not think of my mother as Black and definitely not myself as Black. I am puzzled by and scared of these strange people in my home, and I cannot figure out why they are there. It is only years later I will realize it was my aunts visiting. At the time, I only remember being afraid.

2. My mother doesn't believe in buying dolls. She thinks chemistry sets are a more appropriate toy for making future doctors. But we have a babysitter, and one day she gives my sister and me her old dolls. My sister names her favourite doll Dorothea. She has long, golden hair. When we are older, my sister will tell me that after she was teased at our all-white school for her "witchy hair," she brings in a comb with Dorothea's golden hair tangled into it. She tells the other girls her hair is blond at home, but she has to hide it for school.

Eventually, our cousins visit from New York and they must notice we only have white dolls, so they send us Black ones. I find this doll again later on in adulthood, and I notice I have taken glue and tissue paper and made casts for her limbs. The white dolls' bodies are untouched. I'm not sure what this means — if I hated this doll enough to harm her or if I was trying to care for her, if I wanted to give her visible signs of being fixed somehow.

3. I am five years old and we are painting self-portraits at school. I go to line up to get the pink paint like everyone else, and the teacher tells me I have to wait until everyone else goes so she can add brown to the paint. When she adds the brown, the paint turns a horrible, diarrhea-like greenish-brown and I am forced to paint myself with this. Looking back, I think my teacher was trying to be helpful.

My next teacher uses me as a lesson to the class. There are people in this world who are darker, different than us, she says. Like El.

My Dad is Welsh, and we go to the National Eisteddfod and wear daffodils to school on St. David's Day. So, when my teacher singles me out for being different, I say, that's because I'm Welsh.

4. I am standing with my friend on the corner and an older boy cycles by. Paki! Paki! he yells, coming back on his bike over and over.

I don't know what this means, and I ask Mummy. Your friend wears glasses, she says. He was probably yelling "spec-y."

To this day, I am torn on this story. Most of me thinks my mother was just trying to shield us the best way she knew. Part of me thinks it's possible she really believed this. The story turns on glasses, and I think about them as a symbol of visibility, how my mother tried to save us by substituting the seeing of our skin for quite literally a different lens, a different kind of eye.

This experience actually becomes part of the first spoken word I write: Someone called me Paki. They weren't even good racists!

5. I have been waiting to join Brownies forever because my sister is in it. She comes home and teaches me the songs they sing. Only as an adult do I think about these songs. They sing songs about Hiawatha. They sing a song about "We're from Nairobi, we do the Watusi." They sing a song about "Land of the silver birch, home of the beaver," where the chorus has fake Indigenous singing sounds.

When we actually move to Canada, I join Brownies, and I wear my uniform to school. Someone tells me my uniform is the colour of poo, just like my eyes. Poo eyes, they taunt. That is the last time I wear my Brownie uniform to school.

6. My first memory of racial consciousness is when I am seven or eight and the teacher is reading us a fairy tale, and I notice the good sister always has blond hair and the ugly sisters and witches are always dark. This angers me.

7. I am in competitive gymnastics, and we do an exercise where we are supposed to lie on our backs and squeeze every muscle as tight as we can. Our coach tells us, if your body is tight there should be no space between your back and the floor. Except my body doesn't go flat no matter how much I squeeze.

Later, as an adult, suddenly everyone is into "ghetto booty" and Jennifer Lopez and then Kim Kardashian are being celebrated everywhere, but I remember being in gymnastics and looking at the girls whose bodies were flat all the way down and knowing something was wrong with me. Gymnasts don't have bums or stomachs, our coaches say.

One day I wear spandex shorts to school, and a girl makes fun of me because my butt sticks out. It's funny now, how the same girls who mocked our bodies then are now doing squats and talking about #bootygoals.

8. We go to a cultural festival and there is a steel orchestra. My sister and I want to join but my mother says, The other girls will pick on you. They won't like you because you're lighter than them.

My grandfather was an early pan man. He stole garbage cans and hammered music out of them. He bailed singers out of jail. There is a recording of him in the Smithsonian speaking about calypso history. But I have never learned how to play the pan.

9. I am the golden child in junior high. I get the best grades and I am a star on the track team and I play in band and I volunteer for everything. I win athlete of the year and the prize for highest grade average. I am the only kid who isn't white in the gifted program.

In Grade 9, there is another mixed-race girl in the class, and we become friends. Now, suddenly, when we talk, we get kicked out of class. We get accused of cheating on a test in math class. At the time, I don't understand what has changed, why I am getting in trouble now, why this friendship is so dangerous to my teachers.

In high school I quit track. That year they "accidentally" miscalculate my GPA, and I don't win any year-end awards. My mother is furious with me until my report card comes. Then she sees they have left out a mark completely and averaged the grades without it. She complains to the school. They correct my average, but they never give me the award.

After I quit track, they tell me I won't be able to get a scholarship to university. I am in the AP program and I have no marks less than 90 percent.

At the time, I understand none of this.

10. I take driver's ed, and for the first time I am with students in the "regular" program. My sister goes to a different school, but she takes the class too, and she hangs with the Black girls. They ask her, What's wrong with your sister, isn't she Black? Why doesn't she talk to us? I don't know what my sister says to them.

I walk by the front doors and the Black girls say, What's up, hey, why don't you come over here, what, you think you're too good for us? It's a decade after my mother's sisters coming to the house, but I still don't really understand who I am. Nobody has taught me anything. The only book I can ever remember reading where the characters weren't white is *Underground to Canada*. I remember my mother telling me how the Black girls won't like me. I don't know that I can go over there.

11. My mother once shares with me that she was scared we would turn out "Shabeen," which is a Trinidadian word for people with "hard, red hair."

bell hooks writes about how with white babies the first question is, are they a boy or a girl. But for Black families the first question is, are they light or dark? This will determine the child's chances in life.

My mother also tells me that when I am born, my eyes are slanted and the doctors are convinced I am "mongoloid." I don't know if this is her word or the doctor's. Anyway, my mother has to convince them, That's just how our eyes are; the baby is fine.

My mother grew up in a colonized country. Every sister in her family is aware of where they stand in terms of skin shade. The sister next to my mother was the lightest, light enough to be able to go to a different school. On her first day, a white girl comes up to her and spits on her and says, My mother says she's not going to let me come here anymore now that they let niggers in.

My aunt stops going to school at some point, and Grandmummy is called in. Her sisters are terrified for her, thinking she'll get a beating when Grandmummy gets home. But whatever happened at the school must have been serious, because Grandmummy pulls her out of school and tells her she doesn't have to go back. Nobody ever knows what was said.

My Mummy tells me once that her nursery school teacher made the Black kids play under the table. They weren't allowed out.

My mother's oldest sister was the first Black girl to attend the convent school. They didn't have a choice: on the 11-plus exams she comes third on the entire island, the highest a girl has ever placed. Plus, Granddaddy is Catholic. My aunt loves to sing, but they tell her she can't be in the choir; her legs don't match the rest.

The paper bag test is real — you had to be lighter than a brown paper bag. Mummy tells me the test in South Africa was they had to pass a pencil through your hair. Our parents grew up with this, it's not some ancient history. Breaking down our body parts into specific categories, labelling us, deciding if our nose was too flat past human. My Mummy once says to my sister that the reason why her nose is so flat is because she used to press on it with her own hand when she was a baby. Remember, when they pull over Philando Castile the police report says the suspect has a "wide-set nose."

Understand when I tell you about my mother, don't misunderstand her. Everything she did, everything she said, was about escape, about deep sacrificial love, about not having her children live through the same life she did.

As a child when she told us stories about discrimination, they always had a happy ending. My mum would say, Then I went back and showed them my degree and told them, who's the nigger now? Or she would tell us about our uncle studying medicine in Edinburgh, and how on New Year's Day everyone would ask him to come to their door because it was good luck to see a dark man first thing in the new year. So he would go house to house and get all the food and drinks. She also tells us a "funny story" about how one of our relatives worked in a bakery and the children were convinced the brown bread was his skin rubbing off. Her stories always had a moral: our family was a success, our relatives had triumphed, and nothing could hold us back.

As an adult, I began to think of these stories and ask myself, But *who* said they had to come in a different door? *Who* said her legs were wrong? Why? My mother never told these stories as being about race or racism; they were meant as motivation for why we should get the best grades, to be twice as good to get half as much. But inadvertently, they form the foundation for my racial consciousness, when I think about the systems of oppression that said all the legs in the choir had to match.

I am grateful to my mother for teaching me pride in who we are. That is something I never doubted, not since I was born.

12. I am invited to perform at When Sisters Speak, a showcase for Black spoken-word artists in Toronto. I do my set, and when I come backstage one of the dancers runs up to me. She tells me, Your set was fire! When you started speaking we were all like, who is that? And then we were so shocked — it's the light-skinned girl!

At my first national poetry championship, a white man says nigger from the stage. I am in the bathroom and I walk out just in time to hear him say it. I run back in, announce to my friend, There's a white man calling us niggers! His teammate is in the bathroom and she argues with me that the poem isn't racist, it's about racism. Her Black teammate later tells me that after this encounter, the woman was puzzled about why I was angry. She says, But she's pretty, she could almost be white.

13. I get in an argument with an author. He talks to me about how mixed-race people have it the worst: we experience racism from white people and discrimination from Black people. I say, No, it's because so many mixed-race people carry internalized white supremacy with us from growing up in white communities and families, and that's what Black people are reacting to. They don't hate us because we "have the good hair"; they are objecting because so many of us *believe* we have good hair.

I say, Being mixed-race isn't some special condition. The Egyptians fucked the Phoenicians. The Libyans fucked the Romans. There's been mixed-race kids since the first slave ship departed African shores. It's not some separate condition from being Black; it is the same Black experience. Put me on an auction block in the South in 1800 and see if they sell me, I say.

My mother met my father in a university in Wales. My dad's parents don't attend the wedding in Trinidad. Mummy claims it's just that they didn't like to fly. Maybe that's true. My sister tells me that once she was digging through boxes and she found letters from my grandmother hoping that she wouldn't have "woolly-haired" grandchildren. When we visit, she leaves the house to sleep at the neighbours, but Mummy says it's just because we were loud. It could be. At the end of my grandmother's life, she is convinced there are "gypsies" living in the fields across from her constantly playing music and making noise. Who knows what she felt, really. Mummy writes her every week to the end of her life.

POLICE BRUTALITY BINGO

It's a game that anyone can play
It's on at least three times a day
From Florida to Toronto
It's Police Brutality Bingo

It's in both official tongues
Montreal cops got guns
Just tune into the news
Any channel will do
Twitter and your Facebook page
And if Black people don't wanna engage
You can comment without an intro
Police Brutality Bingo!

So let's review the lingo
Police Brutality Bingo

There's so many ways you can win
As long as you have white skin
If you're ready, we can begin
Just fill the reasons in:
B1, must have run
I2, what did she do?
N3, shouldn't sell CDs
G4, reached through the door
O5, it's their fault they're not alive
Bingo! They're not alive

He had something that looked like a knife
Shouldn't have carried the gun down the aisles
Shouldn't have played with the BB outside
Well, he didn't look like a child
You can play the columns or the rows
Police Brutality Bingo

Well, he had a wide-set nose
Shouldn't have worn those clothes

Shouldn't have worn that hoodie
Should have shown her ID
Should have kept her hands in sight
Shouldn't have asked for her rights
Was probably suicide
Shouldn't have been in that cell
The body cameras will tell
Oops, seems they were erased
Sorry, the footage misplaced
Shouldn't have reached for your phone
Whatever you did, you should have known
Must have done something, the tape cut out
Benefit of the doubt
Even if the police were in the wrong
Only idiots don't play along
Should have shown respect
What do you expect?
And on and on it goes
Police Brutality Bingo!

We can go for the whole card
The police job is so hard
Shouldn't have stolen cigars
Shouldn't have been in that car
He's been pulled over many times
Shouldn't have committed those crimes
I always do what I'm told when I'm stopped
Hashtag all lives matter
Hashtag not all cops

Should have fixed his taillights
Shouldn't speed when you drive
If their parents had raised them right
It's their fault they're not alive
It's their fault they're not alive
Then misuse a Martin Luther King quote
Police Brutality Bingo

From the bottom of the card to the top
How dare you demand no cops?
Just wait 'til you need to call
The number of violent cops is so small
It's not the United States
We don't have the same problem with race
Shouldn't be ruining my commute
Can't support you with that attitude
White people just want to have a conversation
Seems like you just want segregation
Seems like you're the real racist
Why can't you just quietly sit?
It's not the place or time
Why don't you address Black crime?
You shoot each other in Toronto
Police Brutality Bingo!

White people, you can teach your kids
It must be something that they did
There's always something you can prove
Did they reach or did they move?
Were their hands up, did they freeze?
Were they on their back or knees?
Well, then they're threatening you know
It's Police Brutality Bingo

You can get both diagonals
Shouldn't be acting like animals
They're just trying to sue for damages
His body was strong like a savage is
In the middle it's a free square
Their criminal record goes there
It's always good for a smear
You can always rely on white fear

You can always call in a threat
Think how many squares you can get!
He was reading suspiciously long
Must be doing something wrong

Just didn't look like they belong
Better call 911
Nothing to do with me though
Police Brutality Bingo

Whole family can join in the fun
You can pass your racism on
And that's how the cycle runs
It's a game that's never done
You can hang your cards on the fridge
Free square, white privilege
You can put them back when you're bored
Turn off the news report
Put Black people out of your mind
Until you're ready to play next time
That was such a long time ago
It's time to move on, you know
And that's how this whole thing goes
It's Police Brutality Bingo!

CELEBRATING BLACK

Sometimes Black people wonder how we're supposed to
    celebrate
When there's Black life being taken on almost every single date
And any holiday can be turned into a wake
When we're walking on the street or just sitting in our own
    apartment late
White people call 911 on children when they're just selling
    lemonade
At a corner store, a park, a pool party, or parade
And so Black parents tell their children, be careful where you play

Sean Bell gunned down at his bachelor party with his wedding
    the next day
Jemel Roberson wanted to buy his baby Christmas gifts so he
    was working late
Mike Brown executed just weeks after he graduates
Trayvon Martin just buying Skittles
But he walked behind a gate
And that Zimmerman stalked behind him like his Black body was
    bait
Seven-year-old Aiyana Stanley-Jones gunned down in a police
    raid

And when you treat Black life this way
It would be okay if we were filled with hate

But still we pour out love, because it isn't yours to take

So, we still barbecue and dance and laugh and sing and pray
Until some white woman sees us and gets on the phone to say
That we're causing a disturbance and she just doesn't feel safe
But still we keep joying in our being with our bodies taking space

This gift of Black life is from our ancestors' sacrifice
And we won it at a price from the fields of cotton, cane, and rice
On the altar of white profits our bodies were crucified
And they said we were evil darkness and they the sacred light

They told us suffering and slavery would bring us paradise
But here upon this earth we were never recognized

But we have not only survived, we've created and we've thrived
And so we're a living rebuke to white people's appetites
And a reminder of what they despise if they'd ever look inside,
That's a history we write in our sinews, bones, and eyes
Which is why they call police when we're just walking idly by

And that's why tasers, guns, and badges are the power they
    exercise
But our bodies are still here and we are still alive

The names of our martyrs is not something I'll avoid
Tamir Rice was just a little boy outside playing with a toy
Before our seed can grow, they come with weapons to destroy
And still we fill with love that we continue to deploy
We have plumbed the depths of suffering and there we find
    Black joy

So let me say Laquan McDonald, Philando Castile, Rekia Boyd
Andrew Loku, Abdirahman Abdi, Olando Brown, Oscar Grant
Tanisha Anderson, Alesia Thomas, Malissa Williams, Sandra Bland
I can't breathe, choked Eric Garner as he breathed his last
Charleena Lyles was pregnant, her baby never had a chance

We pour libations for the dead as we ritually chant
And their names like seeds on soil become the roots we plant
You see we love each other in our Blackness, though this world
    tells us we can't

And so we'll laugh and shout and praise and barbecue and dance
And we'll welcome in our cousins and our grandparents and aunts
And we'll continue to wear our hoodies and our ball caps and our
    pants
And they'll say that we're no angels in those angry headline rants
But we'll still be filled with pride of being no one can supplant

Though there's Black life being murdered on almost every date
And sometimes we're tired of this burden when we're carrying the
    weight
But let our anger be a stone that causes ripples in the lake
Because we're made of more resilience than anyone could ever
    break
And we're made of stronger stuff than could ever be erased

Cause when you treat Black life this way
We have every right to hate
But we still pour out love
Because it isn't yours to take

ॐ 4 ॐ

No Justice on Stolen Land

A man doing time in federal prison told me he was going to the sweat when a guard called him out of line and challenged him. The guard asked the question familiar to all Black people perceived to be in a place we do not belong: "Where do you think you're going?" ("Can I help you?" is a non-carceral variation of this question when Black people are seen as trespassing.) He pointed to his towel. Where did the guard think he was going? Obviously, the same place as everyone else carrying a towel. The guard determined that he could not be Indigenous. His Black skin was an indelible marker of only one raced identity, and that conception could not fit with the institution's ideas of what Indigeneity is.

This particular policing where Black and Indigenous identities intersect demonstrates the racialized schema underlying colonial ideologies and social organizing. People who are both Black and Indigenous, for example, report having crown attorneys object to their request for Gladue reports: Blackness is categorized outside the ways the courts and colonial systems assign Indigenous identity. Pamela Palmater (2014), Joanne Barker (2008), and Bonita Lawrence (2003) are among Indigenous scholars who have critiqued the specific impacts of the Indian Act upon Indigenous women and the imposition of European conceptions of racialization, kinship, and belonging onto Indigenous Nations. The "settler government's primary policy objective [is] to eliminate Indians," Palmater argues (2014, 29), identifying the historic and ongoing genocide of Indigenous Peoples through proclamation, displacement, dispossession, removal, institutionalization, and particularly through legislating "Indian" identity. Determining and legislating — and eliminating — who is Indigenous is at the heart of Canada's settler-colonial project. Thus, interventions like Gladue reports or limited access to sweats form part of a continuum of state policing of Indigenous identity, coupled with the assumption that Black people illegitimately claim Indigenous status for manipulative or nefarious purposes (prisoners who are both Black and Indigenous point out that white or white-passing participants in Indigenous programs or ceremonies are not similarly policed.) In this way, race-shifting white people are allowed access to Indigeneity, as Darryl Leroux traces in *Distorted Descent* (2019), while any sign of visible Blackness, on the other hand, places you into an impermeable category of Black. When race is used by the state as a categorizing tool, hybridity, fluidity, complex identities, or multiplicity all become challenges to the rigid order and to the accompanying categorization of who needs to be contained, who is a gangster, who is a risk, and what forms of knowledge race supposedly makes legible about a person.

The policing of Blackness out of the sweat also speaks to the ways colonial violences are replicated and repeated — and even intensified — inside institutions. Deliberate population choices by prison administrators create particular sites of racialization in prison. According to Correctional Investigator Howard Sapers (2014), despite an official Population Management Strategy intended to racially integrate prisons, "Black inmates are disproportionately incarcerated in specific institutions in the Ontario and Quebec regions. For example, there are five medium security institutions in Ontario; however, more than half (55 percent) of Black offenders in medium security in Ontario are incarcerated in two institutions (Collins Bay and Joyceville)" (S. 22). While a study by Justin E.C. Tetrault, Sandra M. Bucerius, and Kevin D. Haggerty (2020) demonstrated that prisoners in Alberta "identified with and valued Canadian multiculturalism and subscribed to racial colour-blindness," they also observed that "our participants individualize racism, focusing on what is often called 'overt racism.' Few participants acknowledged 'structural racism' or the overrepresentation of people of colour in the prison system; some even expressed that Canada had overcome racism" (551). It is notable in this study, however, that "Team members [interviewing participants] had varying ethnic backgrounds, though all could be perceived as white" (540). The appearance of interviewers as white and in a position of power and authority as researchers may well have led to prisoners reproducing the discourse of "racial-blindness," as they are expected to, especially in a context where for Black and Indigenous prisoners in particular, expressions of racial pride are viewed by the institution as suspect, dangerous, and gang-adjacent. As former prisoner Tiina Eldridge recounts,

I actually feel a lot of guilt and shame about being brainwashed into being a correctional puppet. I feel I contributed to the reproduction of oppression for others inside and helped to create a need for them to have to enact the same "performances" that I did, in order to be seen as successful and low-risk inmates. (Pollack and Eldridge 2015, 135–136)

In personal conversations, Black prisoners are well aware of the racist prison industrial complex; they are also well aware that speaking about racism gets them labelled as troublemakers, gang leaders, and disruptive elements, leading to them being further contained, transferred, or denied parole. In these "colour-blind" prisons, for example, Black prisoners in Saskatchewan were subjected to what one prisoner calls "cock walks," where prisoners were chained up and forced to walk around naked for the guards' amusement. The prisoner who describes this to me recounts how the guards would specifically target Black men and make comments such as, "If you stacked up all their dicks, they could probably climb over the wall."

Discourses about race and colonization also replicate institutional divide-and-rule tactics; Black prisoners frequently express the idea that Indigenous prisoners have access to services and programs denied Black people. Blackness itself is neither a hegemonic category inside prison nor one of shared unity: being Somali, or Jamaican, or Scotian, or an immigrant versus growing up in Canada, or being Muslim, or being from Ontario, or which African Nova Scotian community you are from all can matter. Fears about being sent "out West" where prisons have high Indigenous populations are also expressed; conversely, Black prisoners transferred from Ontario will complain about the relative lack of Black organization in Atlantic region prisons. I review these complexities because on the outside in abolitionist circles, there is an imagined ideal of Black/Indigenous solidarity that does not necessarily match how people experience and survive prison.

On Prisoners' Justice Day 2020, Yellowhead Institute released *An Indigenous Abolitionist Study Guide* by the Toronto Abolition Convergence. The introduction to the *Guide* states:

In settler states such as Canada, the justice system is an integral component of settler-colonial warfare against Indigenous peoples ... The criminalization, segregation and containment of Indigenous peoples is a deep-seated, ongoing process designed to remove Indigenous peoples from their lands, communities, families, laws, cultures, and languages. Prisons are a colonial imposition on Indigenous lands ... As of late, there has been increased public consciousness around penal abolition and an exciting turn toward the possibility of a world without prisons. We have seen the release of many useful reading lists and guides that provide a sense of the rich history of abolitionist theory and organizing, particularly as informed by the work of Black feminists. *An Indigenous Abolitionist Study Guide* adds to this corpus, gathering together the work of Indigenous organizers and scholars, and addressing the need for an explicitly Indigenous, anti-colonial abolitionist analysis of the penal system. (2020, under "Introduction")

The deliberate framing of the *Guide* in conversation with and informed by Black feminist scholarship points to the ongoing need and possibility for decolonial abolitionist movements in Canada based in this solidarity work. As a slogan repeated often at protests makes clear, there can be no justice on stolen land.

In a conversation between Robyn Maynard and Leanne Betasamosake Simpson reproduced in *Until We Are Free* (2020), Simpson and Maynard emphasize the interconnectedness of Black and Indigenous movements for justice, abolition, and liberation. As Maynard articulates,

We can't fully capture the racial violence institutionalized in the schooling system without also pointing to a long history of residential schools too. The same is true for policing and the broader criminal justice system and for child welfare. Histories of slavery and of settler colonialism and their present realities aren't identical, but they are foundational to this country that we live in ... Sylvia Wynter's work has really helped me think this through, in particular reading "1492: A New World View." The work talks about the founding of the Americas, including the Caribbean, and has helped me really think about the racial logics of genocide and of slavery that were fundamental to the creation of what was called the New World. This laid the foundations for the kind of violence that impacts our communities today. These intertwined histories also help me to think, too, about Black and Indigenous futures. To quote NourbeSe Philip, "make no mistake, if Black lives mattered, or if Indigenous lives mattered, speaking to the two genocides at the heart of the unsettling of the Americas and the Caribbean, we would indeed be living in an altered universe." (2020, 80)

Writing about practices of decolonial resurgence, Leanne Betasamosake Simpson (2017), drawing upon the work of Cherokee scholar Jeff Corntassel, calls upon Indigenous communities to "reject state affirmation, recognition, and the performativity of the rights-based discourse and to move beyond political awareness and symbolic gestures to grounding ourselves and our Nations in everyday place-based practices of resurgence" (192). As Simpson urges, "The generative and emergent qualities of living in our bodies as political orders represent the small and first steps of aligning oneself and one's life in the present with the visions of an Indigenous future that are radically decoupled from the domination of colonialism and where Indigenous freedom is centered" (192). Simpson's praxis of embodiment and resurgence encompasses an abolitionist politic: we must be careful in our theorizing to recognize that while Indigenous scholars may not explicitly name abolition in the same terms as Black feminist scholars, this work must not be erased as forming foundational thinking on liberation, decoloniality, and radical deconstruction of the status quo. It is not the naming that is important but the working toward freedom.

HOW TO WRITE A SETTLER POEM

Write about nature, never about land
Land is political
Land might lead to critical thoughts about land claims
And we just want poems about the rain
Or how we tamed the wilderness
Not about Treaty Rights or fracking
Or who stole this land anyway
Because that might lead to unpleasant feelings of shame
And what are we supposed to do, just give it all back?

So let's just write poems about following the moose tracks
Into the undergrowth
In both official languages
Because Indigenous languages
Don't qualify for a Governor General's Award

And we just can't afford
To think about all those places with Indigenous names
Like, for example, Canada

Definitely avoid poems about race
They don't give awards
To poetry that inflames
Acclaimed Canadian poems are poetry that make us feel safe

Avoid anything that's contemporary or relevant
The words oppression or white privilege just aren't poetic or elegant
And after all Canadian poetry should make you feel benevolent
Like, I'm a good progressive white liberal Canadian and I'm special
Poetry that can be read on CBC and makes you feel intellectual

Being a poetry reader should ideally make you feel
Like you're better
Than regular people
You know it's respectable
If it's boring and ineffectual

Canadian poetry is for settlers
That's why Canada loves nature poems
Because nature is that open sweep of empty space
With no inconvenient Indians
And poetry really should be empty of opinions
Otherwise, isn't it just a rant?

Canadian poetry should evoke a pre-colonial fantasy
Where it's just settlers against the land
And nature is threatening and dangerous
Until it's taken in hand
And conquered existentially by a single pioneering white man
After all, isn't that how Canada began?

Poetry by Indigenous people
Should allow you to place them firmly in the past
It's so sad how those people just can't keep up
With a modern world that's just too fast
Such a gentle people really
Oh, but Idle No More won't last

You should probably appropriate
Some Indigenous images for your own poetry
It's okay, you don't have to ask
After all, famous white Canadian painters
Painted totems and sacred masks

Art is for everybody, after all
That is, until you violate white copyright
But we just do folk art, so it can't be plagiarized
Our ideas and style are available for free
We're not intellectual or anything
It just comes to us naturally

Real poetry is deep
Poetry is spiritual, which means it puts you to sleep
Real poetry should be individual
Real poetry is just about you and your vision

It should be about reflecting on your personal life journey and
     relationships
And comparing that to a fox
It should never be about social justice or collective liberation
Because isn't that just writing in a box?

Isn't that simplistic?
Not sophisticated like, say, poetry about the cottage

Poetry by people of colour is okay as long as it's exotic
Write about spices
White people love that local flavour
Don't write about the racist immigration points system
Or the exploitation of Third World labour

Just write about your grandmother's wisdom or colourful market
     behaviour
White people should feel
Like they're an expert on your culture after reading your poems
So that they can play saviour

Throw in a couple of words in your language
As long as you speak English
When you're around your neighbours
Don't get carried away
Remember, poetry is civilized

Poetry is quiet and white
Just like nature
Nature is the opposite of urban
Which is a synonym for Black
And that means hip hop and slang and loud
And Canadian listeners don't like that
We just want to hear baroque music
And balmy white voices
And poems about your grandmother's farm

Nature is white and calm
Nature is, I get to own a second home in the country

But I'm sophisticated and educated
Not like those rural folk
Nature is, I get to fantasize about being authentic
And getting rid of technology
But not because I'm broke
Nature is, I can give up what I have when I feel like it
Just for fun or a joke
It's not rural poverty or drug addiction or the loss of industry
It's water skiing and campfire smoke

Nature is quiet nights at the cottage
With nothing but the sound of the loons
And loons are on the loonie so that's government-approved
As an image of Canada
Loons are soothing
Really, if you write a Canadian poem
And you can't record it over the sound of loons
Then is it really worth producing?
If you're not writing about nature in Canada
Then what are you really doing?

Write about loons
And not about the Black people they're removing
Or describing the bruising from police brutality
Or how Bill C-51 is attacking our privacy

Write about the lake
Don't write about how we take
Water from the lakes we vacation on
While the reserves who own the lake
Have boil-before-drinking advisories

Write poetry that's already dead and buried in the libraries
Write about the time you saw a deer
Not about how, say, Canadian companies profit off oil in Nigeria

If you're Black, write an update of Shakespeare
That will make white people feel like you're intelligent
And like you admit white culture is superior

That makes them think you're literate
And not like those rappers
Remember, they don't know Black people
Can actually read books with chapters
Write a tribute to Leonard Cohen or the Group of Seven
Or even William Shatner
Definitely don't write poems about the Toronto Raptors
Write about the white spruce, or the white fir, or the white pine

That's why we write about nature in Canada
Because nature is colour-blind

WE BUILT THIS CITY

We built this city
We built this city on land we stole
Built this city
We built this city on land we stole

We built this city on Cornwallis and Britain
We built this city on colonialism
Built on Mi'kmaw land without permission
We built this city with ammunition

And now that it's risen, we build it on prisons
We're building off mental disease and addictions
No industry left so we build on tourism
We're building a city of militarism

And off-record panels inside of the Westin
By Western officials with global ambitions
Build with taxpayer dollars but deny us admission
New defence minister building with MacKay's traditions

We're building on rhetoric of change and transition
While behind closed doors, it's the same old position
We build interventions and armed expeditions
We claim bombing campaigns are human rights propositions

We build up Trudeau, build with liberalism
Same military, same wars, just new government edition
We build while Indigenous women go missing

Build over bagpipes and lobster dinners
And then go home and build nuclear winter

We built this city on capitalism
We build tpp and free-trade propositions
We build Walmarts to push out local competition
Build cheap Chinese goods in sweatshop conditions
We build the economy, global acquisition

Send jobs offshore, unemployment decisions
Used up all the coal, cut the trees, overfishing
Build up the North End, Africville demolition

We're building off poverty, armed forces enlistment
Can't get a job so you get a commission
Build up the shipyards to Irving's conditions
Ships start here, so we're building off wishing
Still building off Harper although we dismissed him
We're gentrifying the projects on that $300 billion

We're building this city on military missions
Building weapons and warships to use on brown children
We build off the blood of Afghans and Libyans
We're building with drone strikes on Yemen and Syrians
Collateral damage, we take out civilians
We build global war over pipeline positions

We're building this city on carbon emissions
We're building a cycle of radicalism
We tortured Arar, extraordinary rendition
We built occupations, just changed definitions

We helped to build ISIS, historical revision
We built Boko Haram to get oil from Nigerians
We build instability, build opposition
We destabilized the Mideast, societal demolition
We build arms trade with the Saudis, geopolitical divisions
We fight proxy wars by our allies' decisions

We're one of the willing, we build coalitions
With the US and NATO and Israeli politicians
We help to build settlements, walls, and partitions
Build an open-air prison in Gaza for Palestinians

We're building in Africa, new colonial mission
Built a security state from the war on terrorism
Cyber surveillance built by government technicians
We built a spy network, the new inquisition

We're building a world where we all are suspicious
We're building two classes of Canadian citizens
We build Islamophobia and hate crimes commission
We build off a racist immigration points system

We build off the tattoo, military tradition
Lockheed Martin on campus helps bill our tuition
We say we're building new weapons to strike with precision
Building new drones with facial recognition
We're building an economy on death and attrition
We're building new treaties on nuclear fission

We build NGOs, then we send in tacticians
We use foreign aid to build imperialism
We build occupations and call it assistance
We build cholera, refugee camps, malnutrition
We build piles of dead bodies and decomposition

We built a new world from 9/11 fruition
We're building this world off of war repetition
The theatre of war is an endless audition
We built Al-Qaeda, we're building militias
We build retaliation, a cycle so vicious
New York, Beirut, Paris, Mali, and Garissa
Military strikes just further ignition

We build global war and there's no intermission
We're building ourselves out of human existence
And we're not bystanders, we're not an omission
Because don't you hear that radio transmission
Don't you remember? Take it back to the beginning:

We built this city
We built this city on land we stole
Built this city
We built this city on land we stole

WELCOME TO CANADA

Welcome to Canada, where you've probably heard
Of lumberjacks in flannel shirts and voyageurs in beaver furs
And don't you know we say eh after every word?
And we've got that handsome young prime minister

They probably didn't tell you about the lack of drinking water on
    reserves
And there's over two thousand missing and murdered Indigenous
    women and girls
They say this is unceded Mi'kmaw territory but fracking still
    occurs
Take a drive down to that statue by the Westin and see the
    history we preserve

Now a majority of people here in Halifax approve
And they say, a statue celebrating genocide of Mi'kmaq shouldn't
    be removed
But then they say, there's no racism here so perhaps you are
    confused
You'd be forgiven if you didn't hear about all the Black kids
    suspended from our schools
Did they tell you about the Colored Home and all the children
    they abused?
Or the solitary confinement that we like to use on youth
And all the Black and Indigenous communities the government
    pollutes

And wait until I tell you about immigration detention and the
    people we refuse
We shackle women to their beds and we say, that's just the rules
Oh, but I saw Trudeau hugging all those Syrians on the news

Ah, did anybody take you to that Tim Hortons drive-through
Well, they hire foreign workers and then threaten to deport them
But when you buy that double double, that's probably not
    important
The UN released a report saying racism here's deplorable

And we're building luxury condos instead of housing that's
    affordable
We just had to settle with Omar Khadr because we allowed him
    to be tortured
We won't let Chelsea Manning come across our borders
But we welcome war criminals who perpetuated slaughters
And people think Canadians are just so polite and so adorable

We love to feel superior and to wave the maple leaf
We're very proud here of our shipyards and all the jobs that
    they've increased
We just don't mention who those warships will be killing in the
    Middle East
Just like we don't talk about the slave money that funded
    Alexander Keith
Don't worry, for a rich person in Halifax he really was not unique
If you committed genocide in Africa, we'll honour you with a
    street
If you were on the side of slaveowners, we probably named a
    university
We were the number one suppliers of salt cod to plantations in
    Haiti
Our merchants petitioned parliament against the end of slavery
And that South End money came from trading with the
    Confederacy
But never mind that history, let's talk about lobster from the sea

You were probably told to try some of our seafood delicacies
Just don't think about the Risley corporation that runs a
    monopoly
They want cameras on the boats of lobster fishermen, invading
    privacy
And we exploit the migrant workers picking our apples and
    blueberries
Nova Scotia is not a friendly province for workers or employees
We've got an anti-union premier in Stephen McNeil
But I doubt the poverty in this province ever makes the highlight
    reel
Lighthouses and bagpipes are probably the only thing you see

And please don't read the comments on Indigenous stories on
    CBC
We've got white supremacist groups interrupting ceremony
They shot fireworks at the water defenders protesting Alton Gas
We tried to pass a motion to ban the Confederate flag
But our police are more concerned about these mythical Black
    gangs
Did they tell you African Nova Scotians were four hundred years
    upon this land?

They promised farms and land grants and then they stole it back
White people change the names of their communities beside us on
    the map
Sidewalks and grocery stores are just a couple things we lack
And now they're investing millions on prison construction contracts

Moving on, you might want to be as careful as a woman taking
    cabs
Unfortunately consent laws are optional for our judges to
    understand
And I know women walking downtown where white men snatched
    off their hijabs
But in we're the land of tolerance, as every Canadian brags

If you're tired of hearing about residential schools and Cornwallis
    taking scalps
Take a walk in the Public Gardens where you can relax
Oh, I forgot about the Boer War monuments to concentration
    camps
And the murderer of Nigerians commemorated on a plaque
Wait a minute, did you hear we were a promised land for Blacks?

Did you drive by our arena named for Scotiabank?
Say that name in the Caribbean and you probably won't get
    thanked
And our money in the region has us joining imperial ranks
The police down in New Glasgow even bought themselves a tank
But say colonialism in Canada and people draw a blank

Because let me tell you about our national sport: we're all fans of
    hypocrisy
I'm sorry, did I get that wrong, I meant to say hockey
And far be it from me to criticize Sidney Crosby
But white people here in Canada? They don't care about Black
    bodies

People are still in denial that this country once had slaves
And police on their patrols are sending Black men to their graves
Indigenous and Black bodies are filling up our jails
They stop us three times more in Halifax, but they say that that's
    not race
It couldn't be, that only happens down in the United States

And if you leave the city over the MacKay bridge
You might want to look out of your window and wave goodbye to
    Africville
And you might hear the cannon firing at noon off Citadel Hill
It's just your daily reminder of all the Mi'kmaq they killed
And the control they have today while the police impose their will
And the elders in our communities are ill from the landfills
And that colonizing slave-trader Queen's still gracing all our bills

And then you turn on US TV and they say, Canada? I heard that
    place is chill
If I could only move to Canada, my dreams would be fulfilled

WHITE JURORS

One white, two white, three white jurors
Four white, five white, six white jurors
Ten white, eleven white, twelve white jurors
It's an all-white jury again

Gerald Stanley walked out of the courtroom a free man
Shots fired through the window of the SUV
They said he was just defending his land
A hangfire, he said, just a twitch of his hand

The life of Colten Boushie worth less than the alleged theft of an
     ATV
What was he doing, was all they debated on TV
Shot to the head while he was lying there asleep
And so, the Indigenous youth was the only one found guilty

And there were comments that he deserved it in a secret
     Facebook group for the RCMP
And a group of Saskatchewan farmers, of course they all agreed
And the publishing companies offered him an exclusive book deal

And the jury pool. Well, the jury pool
It didn't look like me

And there were hundreds of thousands of dollars donated to his
     GoFundMe
Oh Canada, where Indigenous lives still fetch a bounty
For one little, two little, three little

Raymond Cormier walked into court and walked out
Killing an Indigenous girl equals reasonable doubt
The only person on trial was Tina Fontaine
The *Globe and Mail* headline said there were drugs and booze in
     her veins
The cops had her at a stop and they waved her on through
Just like the police asked Colten Boushie's mother if she was
     drunk

When they delivered the news

And the jury pool. The jury pool
It didn't look like you

And while Stanley and Cormier are free as a bird
Adam Capay was held four years in solitary until the time blurred
By the time the ombudsman got to him, he was slurring his words
They said they forgot him, or what even occurred?
They say that's an accident, but haven't you heard?
In federal prisons Indigenous women make up more than one
    third

And over half of the juvenile facilities
And the majority in care who are taken from their families
Just take a walk through maximum security
Or take a look round remand to see who can't afford the surety
And they locked Renee Acoby away into obscurity
But then they tell me white is the equivalent of purity
And since we can't be innocent, we should bow to their authority

We can't win, we can't win
Not when session is in
Not with histories upon histories about savages and sin
If you'll all rise for the jury the court will begin
Selecting *one white, two white, all-white jurors*

You can dress as sexy Pocahontas if you want for Halloween
And Brad Barton was acquitted of murder in the first degree
While Cindy Gladue's vagina was displayed in court for all to see
John Wayne is still an icon of the silver screen
The Birth of a Nation has been a blockbuster since 1915
And there's gated communities where Black folks aren't ever seen
When they stop us on the street, they say that's just routine
And my friend walked into court under a portrait of the Queen

Oh, I tried to buy him suits while the cops showed up in jeans
We worried he'd look guilty if he wasn't cut so clean
They couldn't show any evidence to even place him at the scene

But when it came to read the verdict, you all know what I mean
Thanks to *one white, two white, all-white jury*

And the media? Well, they said from his face they just knew he
    couldn't feel
And now the system tells him that perhaps he can appeal
But in the appeals court, there's
One white, two white, three white judges

We can't win, we can't win
Not when they see a Black skin
And once the door locks, no one can see what happens within
They claim you can try habeas in court, but then the institution
    spins
And who'll believe a criminal and what they have to say?
And now my friend's been there on lockdown twenty-three hours
    a day

And the phone calls only come when your family can pay
And when they have you down in seg the phone doesn't come
    around at all
My other friend broke his leg, and for weeks he had to crawl
And a third's been on a hunger strike three weeks behind those
    walls
They spent money on more weapons getting the guards some
    pepper balls
We claw our way into the halls of justice, but our voice is just too
    small
We can get one or two more judges, but they still write the laws

A guy tried to slit his throat and they just wrapped him up with
    gauze
They released a woman to a bus stop in the winter and said
    that's just protocol
Just like Neil Stonechild and those prairie starlight tours

And there's another woman, another woman, who set herself on
    fire

But when you die in a prison in this province, no one has to
    inquire
No charges pressed for guards who watched Ashley Smith expire
But when prisoners hit the stand, it's them they call the liars

Andrew Loku shot by the police in twenty-one seconds
Fredy Villanueva executed when police said they felt threatened
Sammy Yatim shot on a streetcar when he'd already dropped his
    weapon
But if a cop guns down a Black man, he never has to reckon

We can't win, we can't win
The not-guilty verdict is in
'Cause it's
One white, two white, three white jurors
Four white, five white, six white jurors
Ten white, eleven white, twelve white jurors
It's an all-white jury again

5

Personal Responsibility and Prison Abolition

In the summer of 2020, I was speaking to Jerry over the phone. Jerry is serving life in prison. For the two years I have known him, Jerry has been fighting for access to parole. First, he was transferred to a maximum-security prison on the charge of having kept a store where he sold items from the canteen. Then, his parole officer would not come to see him for months on end. Since you are not allowed to change parole officers, and since his PO was not meeting with him, Jerry was stuck. He tried requests, then complaints, then he considered hiring a lawyer. Finally, despite his fears that challenging the prison would only lead to retaliation, be filed a habeas corpus application, describing how the institution was violating their own procedures. Because Jerry had all the evidence of his complaints and the relevant regulations, the officials immediately agreed to his requests and moved him to a medium-security facility.

By acquiescing at this point the prison officials were not, as it may seem, acknowledging the wrong done to Jerry. Rather, this was a move to prevent his application from being ruled on, a decision that would then set a precedent allowing other prisoners to pursue complaints. The officials were doing what was necessary to prevent any further investigation or criticism of their behaviour: by moving Jerry, they rendered his application moot and avoided the scrutiny of the court. In this case, it worked out for Jerry; more often, when prisoners complain about the conditions of their confinement in a habeas application, the jail will simply temporarily remove the condition — usually a lockdown or segregation — long enough to tell the court the issue no longer exists, and then immediately reinstall the condition once the court has dismissed the application. In this way, they continue to violate the rights of prisoners and dodge accountability with no true avenue for redress. Because the applications are dismissed, no written decisions are issued, making even the documenting of these cases difficult if you are not already aware of their existence or in attendance at court. (For an example of an application deemed moot, see Tim Bousquet's coverage "Habeas corpus hearing illuminates jail conditions" in the *Halifax Examiner* [2018] of an unsuccessful habeas case brought by eight prisoners at Central Nova Scotia Correctional Facility.)

Jerry's problems with parole did not begin or end there. Jerry is convicted of first-degree murder and was given an automatic twenty-five-year sentence. But, as we say, life is life: twenty-five years represents only the first chance at parole, not a release date. Feminist law professor Debra Parkes argues for the abolition of the life sentence (2018), identifying the "punishment agenda" in Canada that includes "not only an increasing prison population, but more fundamentally, a policy agenda that is based on an ideology — often in the face of contradictory evidence — that more punishment (particularly incarceration) will make Canadians safer" (2014, 590). While discussions of prison justice often focus on our reliance upon incarceration as a solution to social problems and the ways policing targets populations deemed outside the notion of "public safety," Parkes also identifies how prison sentences and the conditions inside prisons, such as solitary confinement, become increasingly lengthy and more punitive, including legislative changes to make access to parole more difficult (2014, 592). While many of the policies Parkes describes in her 2014 article came into being under the Harper regime, in 2022 under Trudeau most of these barriers remain despite gestures toward reforms; as Parkes emphasizes (2019), previous governments also enacted tough-on-crime agendas. "Politicians of all stripes have contributed to the expansion of the criminal law throughout Canada's history" (2019, 352), she observes.

While the minimums for life sentences may seem somehow natural and reasonable (you take a life, you get life), as Parkes discusses (2019), the lengthening of life sentences and the decreased ability to achieve parole is actually the result of this punishment agenda that has expanded over time:

> Mandatory minimum sentences appeal in a simplistic way to public calls for safety and accountability for crime. However, they contribute to the mass incarceration of Indigenous people, do not deter crime, and are extremely costly in human and fis-

cal terms. In pursuit of their underlying purpose — to remove discretion from judges perceived to be overly lenient in sentencing — these sentences transfer discretion to the unreviewable charging decisions of prosecutors. Mandatory sentencing laws have proliferated in Canada over the past twenty-five years and until recently, Charter rights have not acted as a meaningful check on governments intent on enacting them. (2019, 359)

For Jerry, what this means practically is that although he received a twenty-five-year life sentence, he is still serving time more than thirty years later. Every time he gets closer to parole, he finds himself transferred, given a higher security rating, facing institutional charges, or denied access to the programs or requirements demanded of him to satisfy the Parole Board of Canada.

I am of no practical help to Jerry. Since I am not a lawyer, a parole officer, or a member of the Parole Board of Canada, there is nothing I can do but listen. I frequently apologize to Jerry for being useless, and he kindly tells me he values the fact that I pick up the phone. At Christmas, he sent me a card with animals on it, since he said I seem like a person who likes cute animals (I am). Once, he said he heard I was a poet, so I read him my poem, "There Will Never Be Justice," about the stories of men doing time. He cried. I do not say that to suggest the profundity of my own work; I imagine when you have a parole officer who won't even visit you, any sign that there are people in the world who care about prisoners and who hear their stories must mean something.

Over that summer, Jerry talked to me about the news and about the discussions he heard and saw about abolition and defunding police. He told me about his own efforts to speak with men inside the prison about abolitionist ideas, and he revealed his frustrations with these conversations. He began by asking what they thought we needed to do to end, or at least reduce, prison sentencing. He said, at first, people's answers largely focused on institutional solutions: more spaces in halfway houses, more programming options, better communications with parole officers. But then, Jerry kept pushing. He asked people to think beyond the assumption that prisons need to exist: What would we do if there were no prisons? He reported to me that this idea was received with skepticism. People pointed to dangerous offenders and argued that we need prisons to contain them. People suggested that they themselves were repeat offenders, and without prison they would go back to committing crimes. Some people offered solutions like electronic monitoring or chemical castration for sex offenders, but Jerry told me nobody was on board with the idea that prisons could be obsolete.

Jerry was annoyed by these responses and, as he described it, the lack of political analysis. These men, under the heavy boot of state oppression, continued to believe that the state punishes in a just way, that prisons reduce crime and address harm, and that bad people must be punished. But their response was not surprising to me. One reason is in the ways carceral institutions insist upon particular expressions of responsibility and remorse. As Patricia Monture (2006) observed about how the work of the Task Force on Federally Sentenced Women was taken up by Correctional Service Canada (CSC), focus is continually shifted away from historical and systemic injustice — including the effect of colonization, racism, poverty, and ableism on criminalized people — and onto the notion of a "criminal mindset" chosen by the "offender." In Monture's example, the framework of "creating choices" was intended as a

> philosophical attempt to shift the gaze from a system that corrects to one that collectively empowers women. This was an attempt to move women's corrections to a place that constructed women's criminal offending as a mere reflection of gender oppression in Canadian society (CSC 1990, 16, 25). It was an attempt to relocate the power to make choices in their lives out of the hands of prison officials and back to the women themselves. (2006, 28)

Instead, CSC used the notion of "choices" to responsibilize women for their own offending, recharacterizing women as "dangerous" (2006, 29); securitizing the prison space through fences, razor wire, and enhanced surveillance; and "re-entrenching the legitimacy of prisons to punish and coerce" (30). As Monture also notes, these constructions of danger particularly affect Indigenous (and Black) women; and indeed, thirty years after the Task Force, Indigenous women represent 42 percent of federal admissions in Canada (Office of the Correctional Investigator 2020).

These demands for personal responsibility for crime structure the programming prisoners must take to fulfill their correctional plans and be eligible for parole. John P. McKendy (2006) analyzes the effect of this programming on preventing prisoners from even accessing language about their own trauma or humanizing themselves. As McKendy observes,

> Now more than ever, the official institutional frame of the prison screens out sociologically oriented accounts, i.e., ones which bring into view the external forces that shape and condition the behaviour of the individual. The linchpin of the discursive environment of the prison has become the self-possessed, "responsibilized" individual, the individual enlisted in the process of his own control. (2006, 475)

McKendy is critical of the responsbilizing of crime and the "banishment" of prisoners' stories. He argues that, since prisoners face sanctions "for straying from the lineaments of the institutional discourse promoted and enforced by the prison staff and administration," they are forced to "go along with the construction of [themselves as] responsible agent[s]," which "may make [them] into a kind of person that [they are] unable or unwilling to recognize" (2006, 479). McKendy performs discourse analysis on the stories of the men, identifying the ways they interrupt themselves to cut off stories of their own trauma or other exculpatory factors to insert the CSC-approved rhetoric of guilt and choice. He suggests that these demands may impede the desired rehabilitation, as it forces the men's experiences into contours of shame, culpability, and "badness" that might prevent them from coming to terms with their harm in healthy ways. Even their speech has been colonized and infiltrated, and in turn they lose access to the language to name themselves, their own stories, and their own lives. McKendy concludes by observing,

> Imprisonment involves not just physical confinement, but also discursive or ideological confinement. What men in prison are prompted to say, the sorts of discursive opportunities they are afforded, the kinds of stories that are officially ratified — all of these are severely restricted. (2006, 497)

As Jerry observed, these narratives of responsibilization make it impossible for many prisoners to think beyond prison walls. Asked to imagine a world where prisons did not exist, they could only return to more effective ways of enacting punishment. Although they are themselves prisoners, they upheld the category of prisoner as normal and needed, supporting that designation by pointing to their own crimes as examples. If prisons worked, surely they would not be repeat offenders, but that cannot emerge in this discourse; instead, the very failure of the prison system to address the roots of crime becomes proof of its necessity. As criminologist Tamari Kitossa (2020) demonstrates, "authoritarian criminologists" reify the ontological fiction of "crime" in service of the "ruling relations of ableism, capitalism, colonialism, hetero-patriarchy, and white supremacy" (8). Crime, writes Kitossa, is

> a rhetoric whose practical function is to enable domestic pacification of the citizen-herd by economic, military, and political elites — in short, statecraft is a protection racket, a veritable regime of violence consisting of extortion, extraction, deprivation, lies, threat, and the breaking of bodies. (2020, 11)

The fiction of crime produces the fiction of a criminal, which in turn produces the fiction of the prison as a place for bad people, which then demands that those inside agree with their own categorization: to be criminalized is to be forced to agree that you are a criminal.

As Lisa Lowe (2015) observes, the archive of the liberal state "subsumes colonial violence within narratives of reason and progress" (2). In the prison context, archiving is made even more difficult by the multiple silencings that prevent records from even being kept. Prisons are both over-recorded when it comes to the constant surveilling of prisoners and the keeping of reports and files (a practice I have termed the "violence of the paperwork" for the ways the nation state uses bureaucratic practices and structures to both enact and disappear violence), and simultaneously under-recorded when it comes to documenting claims of abuse by losing complaint forms; rendering applications to the courts moot to prevent written decisions; transferring prisoners who complain; and removing prisoners to solitary confinement where they cannot contact family, friends, or even lawyers. These moves to silence prisoners are framed as reasonable interventions that preserve the security of the prison. Prisoners are thus trapped in a cycle of paperwork, which in turn forces them to continually engage in a performance, a charade of fair process that they always and already know is stacked against them and doomed to fail. Thus, placements in solitary confinement are "reviewed" only to conclude their continued placement is necessary, or it is their behaviour that is at fault and not the prison disciplinary system; complaint forms must be endlessly submitted only to submit further complaints about the ignoring of the previous complaints; prisoners must attend disciplinary hearings with no legal representation that inevitably end in their punishment, and so forth (Jackson 2002).

Prisoners' attempts to secure their rights or protect themselves must engage with and extend the systems oppressing them in the first place. This is the problem of abolitionist engagement as well: to do the work that supports people in prison, we must fund the prison industrial complex by paying money for phones, sending in funds for canteen, and otherwise supporting the very institutions we wish to abolish. Similarly, Parkes' work (2014, 2018, 2019) frequently demonstrates the failure of law to advocate for prisoners: Parkes advocates for the law as a possible instrument for prisoners to receive redress while simultaneously recognizing the liberal fiction that the law acts as a check to injustice wielded by the state, and not as its instrument. It is no coincidence, for example, that virtually every civil rights movie is set in a courtroom, sending us the message that if the state makes mistakes, it is also the only site where these mistakes can be corrected. For Monture (2006), the efforts of Indigenous women to craft a different frame for women's prisons were co-opted and twisted. In both women's work, then, we understand the barriers abolitionist thinking repeatedly meets with on all fronts of the criminalizing system.

Meanwhile, within the prison, arbitrary and unaccountable disciplinary systems, like those Jerry experienced, operate beyond the courts and outside legal representation to repunish prisoners. These internal systems, as demonstrated by Howard Sapers (2014), target Black (as well as Indigenous [Office of the Correctional Investigator 2012]) prisoners based on subjective judgements of gang membership, disobedience, and threat based in anti-Blackness. Prisoners, then, in all sites at all times experience a reinforcement of their stigmatized, subordinate, captured state, in which only expressions of obedience, submission to prison authorities, and acceptance of sin provide a path to freedom. Is it any surprise, then, that abolitionist thinking does not flourish in these spaces?

Prison lawyer Michael Jackson (2002) reminds us that crises are actually part of the life cycle of institutions, allowing the institution to enter a phase of reform, which in turn allows it to extend and continue. In *Justice Behind the Walls*, Jackson (2002) recounts the many crises and accompanying reports and inquiries that have punctuated the Canadian prison system, concluding with his student Ori Kowarsky that rather than provoking change, crisis is indeed crucial to the resiliency of the system. This cycle of paperwork, inquiry, complaint, review, application, law, committee, task force, etc. all serve to prop up the prison, trapping prisoners within it (Razack 2015). If prisoners cannot see beyond the prison, it is perhaps because, practically, there is no "beyond" in a sealed system that tells prisoners the very law that condemns them is the law that will somehow free them, as if that law can be separated from its colonial, racist, patriarchal roots.

Perhaps another reason why the prisoners Jerry talked with were not abolitionists is because of the relative lack of abolitionist literature and discourse centred on Canadian prisons. To make matters worse, the majority of the writing that does exist is largely in an academic frame, and neither directed at, nor produced for, nor developed with people who are incarcerated. Rather than beginning with the prisoners and moving outward, as Jerry's work with his fellow prisoners attempted to do, more often these ideas gain the most currency outside of the prison space completely. This is not to say that prisoners are not agents of their own liberation. For example, Prisoners' Justice Day — begun by prisoners in Millhaven Institution on August 10, 1975, in remembrance of Edward Nalon who bled to death in his cell the year before — is commemorated every year by prisoners accompanied by fasts and striking from work (lilley 2014). As pj lilley's "retrospective montage" collects, Prisoners' Justice Day is a rich source of art, writing, and political protest. Another example of historic and influential documenting of prisoner organizing is Claire Culhane's work spanning two decades of correspondence with over a thousand incarcerated people from 1976 until her death in 1996. Culhane's model of advocacy included not only writing but offering direct help with grievances, staging sit-ins, picketing Parliament Hill, and visiting prisons. Her book, *Barred from Prison: A Personal Account*

(1979), recounts how, after helping to negotiate a prison riot, Culhane was banned from BC Pen and then all but two federal prisons in BC and all provincial ones for the supposed safety of the institution. Despite this rich history of prisoner organizing, work on prisons in a Canadian context often looks to the United States and relies upon US-based texts, resulting in a comparatively short body of these works in Canada.

One project that attempts to remedy this absence is the *Abolition in So-Called Canada Syllabus* (2020). The *Syllabus* creates an important intervention into discourses both of incarceration and of abolitionist thinking and praxis that centre the United States, while viewing Canada as the lesser actor when compared to US state violence. Far from being a simple book list, the *Syllabus* foregrounds the act of collecting. In gathering the *Syllabus* as a communal act, the document simultaneously builds capacity, solidarity, and mutual investment in abolitionist practice. I sent one of the draft versions of the *Syllabus* while it was being circulated on the email listserv to Randy Riley, who was completing sociology courses while incarcerated; unable to access a computer for extended periods of study time, the document allowed him to complete the annotated bibliography required for a term paper. These living documents facilitate the work of an abolitionist like Randy, who as a wrongfully convicted African Nova Scotian man currently does his work from behind bars, generating the ground for future abolitionist theorizing.

I want to position this *Syllabus* to remind us that Randy's work is, for example, speaking with the white kitchen staff who work at the prison and encouraging them to understand that the building of prisons will not solve the economic conditions in their communities. As one of the authors of the statement, "Black Lives Matter in Prison Too," he wrote,

> Prisons are built in small rural towns. Recently, in a conversation with one of the workers, she told us she was in favour of the prison being built because it would offer jobs. When she was told about the conditions and that we do not have programs or any rehabilitation, she was shocked.
>
> We want to send a message to people who believe that building a prison in their community will stimulate the economy. Prisons are not a retirement plan or social security. Putting money into prisons is not a solution to poverty or to any social problems. We ask people living in these communities to

reject spending money to put more people, especially Black and Indigenous people, into prisons. ("Black Lives Matter in Prison, Too" 2020, n.p.)

Randy was also one of the main organizers of the Black August Burnside prison strike, organized by prisoners in Central Nova Scotia Correctional Facility in 2018 in solidarity with the prison strike begun in the United States. He organized prisoners to protest predatory phone charges while serving time in Northeast Nova Scotia Correctional Facility (Devet 2017) and is a co-founder of the *Black Power Hour*, a radio show collective with prisoners airing on CKDU 88.1 FM in Halifax and uses the radio as a platform to organize, support, and liberate prisoners. Randy is generating both the literature and the action that is Black-focused abolition in Canada: an abolitionist praxis that we must remember so often takes place in the space of the unpublished and unnamed. Even as abolitionists challenge state power — and capitalist and colonial relations both within the state and in our personal interactions that reproduce these hierarchies — we must be mindful that who has access to power and platform continues to be informed by the same power relationships we work to dismantle.

Interludes

Music and movement

Every liberation campaign we do, we choose a playlist. After Randy's conviction, Reed and I choose "Glory" by Common and John Legend as our theme song, for keeping the faith. "One day when the glory comes, it will be ours … one day when the war is won," the chorus goes.

For Elmi, it was "Stronger" by Chezidek. "They cannot break me, they cannot shake me. Stronger, I'm stronger, stronger than they know."

I went to a talk at the law school with Sean MacDonald and Glen Assoun. Glen spent almost seventeen years in prison and then four more years on restrictive bail conditions. Even when he was out but still waiting for his exoneration, the stress was so intense that he had a mental breakdown. And all the while, the file was sitting on Jody Wilson-Raybould's desk. This casual neglect, it's almost a theme by now.

During the talk, Sean plays audio of Glen being dragged out of court. Glen was forced to represent himself. During the trial, he turned to the jury, pleaded with them. I'm innocent, he told them. The judge yells at him to stop addressing the jury, and when he keeps speaking, the sheriffs place their hands over his mouth and drag him out of court. Sean asks Glen how he felt in that moment. "I felt less than human," Glen says.

There's these words in *Macbeth*: "Tomorrow and tomorrow and tomorrow. Creeps in this petty pace from day to day to the last syllable of recorded time." That's what describes this work, this holding on. Long periods of time where you can do nothing but wait. Hope is the enemy. I try to imagine nothing. The worst part is, you start to only think of the person behind bars, as if they belong there, as if we should get used to this.

Bus stops

Every so often when I'm waiting for the bus, a woman will come up to me smiling, and I look at her, and it's a woman I wrote with in the women's prison, Nova Institution. We always hug, laughing and beaming at each other, the human contact and joy we were forbidden when we sat together at those glass tables, when even talking too much about your lives at all or any affection was cause for suspicion.

One time I was waiting in the visiting area for the women to come down, and I got up and looked through the books and games and magazines on the shelves for visiting families and I found a sheet of paper. A mother had made a list with her children of what she would do when she got out. Order pizza, it said. Talk for as long as I want with no one listening. One of the entries said, Walk, not in a circle.

One of the women goes into a long meditation once on the phrase "on the outs," about how it can mean you're angry with someone but then it also means what you hope for. I'll see you on the outs.

On a hot summer day, I'm running up and down Citadel Hill, focused inside myself. There's construction on the road around the hill, and a woman is there holding a sign. After a few repeats, when I get to the top, she comes over to me and asks me if I used to come to Nova. We chat for a minute at the top of the hill, a metaphor come to life, she has climbed this far, she made it out.

Pen boxes

Randy's pen boxes are a total nightmare. He has lots of people who love him, but we can't get it together. I mean that literally and metaphorically. People get sick, I'm in and out of town, we're just not organized. He has to keep putting in extensions. You're only allowed the five boxes of all your clothes, electronics, kitchen stuff, workout gear, books, music, and then nothing for the rest of your time. If you're doing life, you're supposed to wear the same stuff at the end of your sentence that you got going in, no matter how much styles change, no matter how much your body changes, no matter how worn out.

When we finally get the boxes together, though, everyone has gone all in. You're allowed two pairs of sneakers; he has five. Dozens of t-shirts. Over a dozen jeans. All brand name. Love will always show itself no matter how much they try to stomp it out. Of course, he can't have all of it, you have to stick to the list, but this excess is a form of resistance too.

Nursing

Martha Paynter and I are presenting at a nursing conference. I'm just doing poetry, but Martha is talking about pregnant mothers in prison, how babies miscarry, how mothers labour for hours in their cells while other women scream for help, a breech foot sticking out of a woman's vagina suspected as contraband, visits to the doctor's appointments in orange and shackles. I have put it in a list, just like that, just like I could list off the names of deaths in custody, just like I could list the reports and inquiries, the way we think listing is knowing and knowing is seeing.

And how do you witness, anyway? Desmond said to me when we were having a conversation about statistics that slavery was also the biggest statistic-gathering exercise on Black people, and it's not like that was about freedom. I like to imagine sometimes that two hundred years from now, people will look back on us and try to imagine us, a backward, dirty people, the way we think about others in history. How could we tolerate doing what we did. I want to be the monster for someone a long way away, some *Star Trek* future world where everything is just good and clean, but we don't know how we got there. In the here and now, we have to fight in messy ways, asking ourselves what right we have to lay out other people's suffering to rooms of eyes, asking ourselves for dignity and humanity and compassion and kindness, describing this horror, oh, it's happening right now.

Afterward a woman who nurses in a jail comes up and says that a guard asked her if it would damage the baby if he had to pepper-spray a pregnant woman. Claire, I think it is, tells the nurse maybe she should tell him it would lower his sperm count permanently.

Writing

The first time I go into a prison, writer and activist Ardath Whynacht invites me for a poetry workshop with the women in Nova Institution. Afterward, driving back from Truro, she tells me that one of the women whose poetry I really loved was convicted of a notorious crime. She doesn't know if I realized it or not, wants to make sure I'm okay, that I'm not going home upset. I think about it and tell her, when you're doing poetry together you don't think about what the person did, you think about their words. Ardath says something that will stick with me for years: I wish I could find the same forgiveness for people in my life that I do for the people in here.

A couple of years later, I am teaching Dante's *Inferno* and we do an exercise where I ask students who they would put in hell. Some of them name this woman, the one who wrote the poetry.

Equality

When I was allowed to go into the max unit to write with the women, we would meet in a room used for school, programs, the library, and activities. One day, I'm meeting with the women one on one, and we don't have enough paper. We start writing on the whiteboard in the room instead. The woman I'm writing with tells me about how she was trafficked and held in a motel room for weeks, kept naked and drugged. She finally escaped. She described running through the lobby of the motel, barely knowing where she was.

The cops gave her a few thousand dollars and put her on a plane back home. That was it. She told me she spent the money on drugs, and when she ran out, she robbed a pharmacy. She got five years, more than the men who kidnapped, raped, and abused her ever served.

On the board in the room, she writes about running, and about healing and hope. I tried to memorize the poem, to hold onto it before it was erased, but it's gone from me, like a shape moving indistinctly behind a heavy door.

Anonymity

Some people on the radio don't say their names. Maybe it's to protect themselves legally. Maybe it's because they know there might be backlash. Sometimes I think it's also the chance to talk to someone for a minute who doesn't know, the chance to have someone on the other end of the phone whose voice isn't coloured by knowing their crime. Maybe those moments feel a little bit closer to what it might be like to be forgiven.

Memory

For years we've been saying that so many of the women in prison have traumatic brain injury from abuse. Years of being thrown against walls, bounced off floors, slapped, stomped, crushed, punched, they do damage. Women struggle to remember appointments, to keep time straight. Then in their files they're written up as unreliable, disobedient, careless.

Do you remember me, the women always ask when I see them on the outside. I think they're also asking, did you see me. Was I a person to you.

Choices

When we advocate for people in prison, we try to say the things that will make people sympathetic. We talk about non-violent offenders, people with mental illnesses, first-time offenders. We tell the stories we think will allow people to see those in prison as human beings, as suffering beings. We say things like, The majority of people in prison are convicted of non-violent crimes, or Over 80 percent of women in prison are victims of sexual and physical abuse. These things are true. But then, what happens when we are working with the people who have committed violent crimes, the people who are the abusers? Are we saying then they are not part of our fight against injustice, or that our advocacy doesn't extend to them? Are we admitting they are beyond the pale, outside of what is acceptable to care about or speak for or even to just not recoil from?

I believe we have to advocate for justice and human rights for everyone. That sounds like an empty kind of statement, but it is actually a bedrock belief, which I understand I feel only because I had to think and work through what it meant to also work with violent people. I can't say, justice only for the people who are sympathetic. Rights only for the people we like. I can't choose who the "good" people are. So, I believe with all my heart we fight for justice for everyone; we advocate for humane conditions because human rights are not only for who we decide is deserving. Because who can decide that? Well, you can say, what about serial killers, obviously. But then there's murder, and manslaughter, and assault, and gangs, and weapons, and sex offences, and dangerous driving, and drug dealing harms communities, and stealing harms businesses, and someone is always going to have a different boundary, a different line, a different experience. I don't believe we can pick and choose justice and include some people and not others.

Headlines

Early on in doing the show, I read in the paper about someone whose name I recognize, and they have been designated a dangerous offender. The article describes what they did. It is horrible. I have talked on the phone a few times to this person; they like to make requests. I tell a friend of mine inside how bothered I am by reading this. When the man is being sent to federal, my friend tells me, I know you don't like him. But he always shared his food with me, always looked out for me. So when he was leaving, I went up to him, and I just said, keep your head up and shook his hand. I think about this for a long time, about how sharing food doesn't change what this person did, but when you're doing time with people, those kindnesses also make a difference. I think about what that complexity means, and I come to see that of course I am bothered, sickened, and also being bothered doesn't change the work I do or the need for it to be done.

Usually with the big headlines, I know or have talked to the person behind them. It's a small community inside prison. Especially if the accused person is from the Black community, then I probably also know the victim's family or people who are grieving and hurt by the crime. Sometimes I know the victim. I've sat with family members and ached with their profound grief, and then taken a call from the person who caused that.

I see the devastation. I don't ignore it. But I also know that the person arrested, I might be talking to that person for at least the next couple of years. And I'm going to come to know them, and I'll see them differently.

Sometimes the people I know in prison also know the victim. Sometimes they are grieving too. Maybe they caused harm to someone else themselves. It's not just messy for advocates; the people inside are affected too. We like to imagine that criminals and victims are separate people, but it's not like that at all. People who have been victimized commit crimes. People who have been incarcerated become victims. People from high crime communities also come from high victim communities. You might be friends with killers and family to the dead. We'd like it all to be tidy and put away nicely, but it doesn't work like that.

The headlines feel painful, I just said. It's more than that. Sometimes I think this work doesn't bother me, and I hear tragic stories all day and listen and comment calmly. And then I wake up at night with anxiety just vibrating through my body, and I don't know why. This is a legacy of that terrible buildup, when I sat through a trial and every day my body didn't know what it was waking up to, what awful thing, what sadness, what pain would I encounter today. So my body woke up on alert, braced against the stress and the horror. And now that lives in my body and people's stories leak out of me as I lie in bed for hours, shaking, when they have nowhere else to go.

Absorption

It's not about making choices between the person accused and the victim or their family, but it can feel like it is. When you have relationships with people in prison, it can feel like you absorb their guilt by proximity. If you support them, or laugh with them over a joke, or advocate for them, or listen to their words, or even just take their call, are you implicitly saying you don't care about the victim or about the harm done? You can feel responsible for what they did, like it rubs off on you.

But feeling that guilt is also about the stigma of prisoners, the idea that any contact with them diminishes or contaminates us. The stigma against prisoners is so powerful that when we go against it, as mothers or children or family members or friends or partners or advocates, it's like we cross over too, like we become part of the "other" side of society. And that makes it frightening for people to think about people in prison or challenge how we feel, the fear that we'll become "other," that it makes us "for" murder, or violence, or harm.

I learn to negotiate these difficulties too by learning from the people in prison. They have to live in difficulty, negotiate every day their relationships with people who are guilty of things they may be bothered or disgusted or hurt by. Especially in provincial jail, where people serving time on crimes like fraud or stealing or breaches can be there with someone awaiting a murder trial.

Sometimes it's not about profundity but just about getting through the day. Maybe the person next to you always has canteen food, or maybe they can translate for you, or maybe you just don't want problems, so you figure out how to get along. Just because we're in here doesn't mean we don't have morals, people often say to me. We know wrong from right. It's not about condoning, it's about figuring out how to live together. And in doing that, I watch them and learn lessons for myself about the futility of judgment in this work, and I learn about how to live in spaces beyond judgment.

Jobs

One time, I told someone inside I didn't get a job I badly wanted, and he said, They probably know you're down with criminals. People hate us, and if you're down with us, they'll hate you too. I don't think that was the reason, but he did. He told me it would be okay if I didn't talk to them anymore, to save myself.

Nicknames

One guy tells me, when he got convicted, he came back to the range and everyone started calling him "killer." It bothered him a lot, but he couldn't show that. And he had to learn to embrace it in some ways, just to survive what was ahead. Everyone watches the news, reads the papers, knows the details, has feelings about it.

Mixed feelings

One woman did time with a woman convicted of murder, who was later killed. She says, I looked out for her for months. If I saw her now, I'd punch her in the face. She says to me, She stayed with me a couple of times. I was friends with her before she was killed, I miss her every day. Maybe I would have been next. Then she talks to me about the pictures in the news, and how they probably wouldn't choose nice ones for her if she died. You know the pictures they normally choose for junkies, she says.

Another woman says, She was my friend. She sat with her for eight months. People don't know the whole story, she says. She talks about women in abusive relationships, her own experience. You don't know what's inside people, she says. She says it's not about agreeing with what she did, but they were close inside and she's not going to forget that either. Someone calls her a "psycho bitch." If you support that, you're sick, they tell her.

It's not an easy thing to work through for anyone. Everyone is talking about it, processing it with each other, and trying to figure out how they feel. We don't think about this part, how people inside, the people who will live with the headliners for the next decade, how they make sense of things, how they work through their own trauma, how they think about forgiveness or tolerance or accountability. We believe in prisons, but we never think about what it means to live there. This difficulty is part of life.

When you do advocacy work with people in prison, there aren't going to be easy conclusions. Nobody who does this work doesn't think about these things, how we negotiate our own feelings about crimes. Some people draw specific boundaries. I know some people who won't work with sex offenders — sometimes they've been assaulted themselves and they don't feel they can do the work for justice and advocate effectively. Some people feel uncomfortable and they just don't want to. Some people feel uncomfortable but do the work because people are going to be back in our communities, and if nobody has even tried to help or offer supports or programming, what then? And some people make the decision to work with everyone no matter what, as long as they want and need programming or supports.

Grey areas

The truth is, we struggle with these questions every day. We wouldn't be human if we didn't. That complex work of humanity is so much a part of prison advocacy. We often don't talk about that struggle and reflection and doubt because we are speaking so urgently about issues we feel are important, and because we want to speak strategically, and also, I think, because dealing with the grey areas is so complicating and when you're still trying to get people to see things like shackling a critically ill woman to her hospital is bad, or putting people in solitary confinement for four years is inhumane, you're still trying to deal with the most basic issues of prison justice. So, talking about negotiating how you feel about horrific crimes or questioning yourself, or the internal dialogues around why you do what you do can seem like it's introducing a harmful doubt. Because these are the crimes that make people support prisons, and the ones that make people accuse, So you want these people running the streets? It's cases like this that convince people we need prisons, and punishment is cathartic, so we try not to talk about them and talk about the easier ones.

But advocacy isn't about being perfect. It's actually about these struggles and negotiating them and working them out. It's not just about the black-and-white cases and the cases everyone empathizes with, the stuff that we all agree upon. It is about challenging how we think and feel about the difficult issues and being honest with ourselves about those feelings.

After

One of the women asks me, Would you still take their calls? And all I say is, It's open to everyone. We don't make those decisions. She says, I wouldn't pick up. But I guess that's what you guys do. I guess you have to.

I hear he asked what I thought, if I read it. I wonder about that, how he didn't show remorse, but then he worries about what I might think of him. I'm not God, I say to the person who asks me, meaning it's not my judgment to make. Meaning, also, we have to be committed to building unconditional spaces for people in prison if we want to share in this work, create agency, build connection. I think the person asking me what I think is also testing me, seeing how I might feel about him, seeing if I'm disgusted by people inside, really, or if they can count on supports still being there. They have to trust we won't take things back, turn away, stop talking to people like they are human beings.

Phone calls

M. calls me. He can't talk long; he's only got a few cents left on his phone. He just wants me to know, the next time I hear from him, he'll be out. As the phone starts cutting off, I say, next time in freedom. I get off the call and start tearing up.

J. has been gently teasing me for a while about poetry. Information gets around in prison. People know things about me I haven't told them — I'm a vegetarian, I run. I ask J. if he wants to hear a poem. He says okay, and I read him the one about all the stories of people doing time. He's thirty years in, so I'm nervous. I know he'll be able to detect any bullshit. To both of our surprise, when I finish, he's crying. I think it's just knowing someone's out there listening, and trying, even when nothing happens.

Voices

On the show, the callers say, Thank you for giving us a voice. To the listeners out there, just because we're in here doesn't mean we don't have something to say. One of the women calls in from the outside and talks about a documentary she participated in when she was inside. When she got out, they filmed her as she was leaving. All the women were banging on the windows as she walked away. Shout out to all my girls in there, she says.

And this is how we go on.

THERE WILL NEVER BE JUSTICE

I know a man who stabbed a man inside and got sent off to the
    SHU
But he says when somebody comes after you, then what else do
    you do?
I don't believe he's a monster, but that's what the system say
And now he's doing double life and might not see the light of day

And when you're fifteen and your family teaches you to sell crack
Well, is there any coming back? So you grow to manhood in the
    max
And we define entire lives by a person's worst acts
We just list their various crimes and believe we have the facts

So here's another story of another lost defendant
He's twenty years old and he's eight years into his sentence
Brought over to the prison from juvenile detention
Sometimes children in this country, they just don't deserve a
    mention
Until they commit a crime and then suddenly, we pay attention

There are people in society we label as disposable
When you're already doing time, shouldn't be the first time you're
    diagnosable
So we put them in a prison where at least they are controllable
And I suppose it isn't notable and no one gets emotional
Unless we find out they are innocent, then maybe humanity's
    negotiable

But for the rest, you did the crime so your humanity's ignored
And men are in so long they don't know how to use a door
And men are in so long they've never heard of Internet Explorer
That's what happens when you're Black, when you're Indigenous
    or poor
When you're considered to be a criminal before you're even born

I get an incoherent call at three o'clock in the morning
The same guy who called me, crying to report he was assaulted

He says he's locked up in his room surrounded by guns and knives
If they come to take him back it's either his or their lives
He says ever since he left the prison, he's been numbing with a
    high
But people say to close his mouth because it doesn't happen to
    real guys

I suppose it's ironic he's from the same reserve as Donald
    Marshall
It seems to me that justice there was only ever partial
When we look back at that case and say, those eleven years
    were awful
But for everybody else the same suffering is lawful

I've heard so many tragic stories I could almost tick off a box
But still we call it justice when the prison doors are locked

We believe that punishment comes to the people who deserve it
But punishment mostly comes to the people who can't swerve it
Can't avoid it, can't employ it, can't voice it, can't afford it
And then once you go to prison, whatever happens, can't report it

So we talk about wrongful. But what are the rightful convictions?
Sure, there's Paul Bernardo, Clifford Olson, Robert Pickton
But what about the man on his fiftieth charge of shoplifting?
When it's obvious to everyone the problem is addiction
And the Truth and Reconciliation Commission can only be a
    fiction
As long as Indigenous people are still filling up the prisons

I have a hard time seeing justice as a reserve without a well
But then we bring its children a smudge kit in their cell
Don't we wonder what will happen when there's foster kids living
    in hotels?
Or Black children in the principal's office five minutes past the
    bell
Because they never learned to read, and they fell between the
    gaps
We start with zero tolerance by the time they're done taking
    naps

Is it justice when some people start the race ahead by laps?
In a country where we can't even guarantee clean water from the
    taps
And there's Indigenous land under every prison on the map

As you move up from minimum to medium to max
It's a funny thing in Canada, how the skin just gets more Black
And lack of access to parole that is kind of like a tax
A couple years of extra sentence that they tack on to our backs
And there's those weapons laws they pass, they claim they're for
    the gangs
While there's white supremacists in prisons with KKK upon their
    hands
And then there's guards who give them daps

And the police can gun down teenagers and never hit the stand
I won't even get into asking why we never charge the banks
But should anyone be sent to where they have to carry shanks?
I watch police roll into Ferguson with snipers riding tanks

I don't think you have to not have done it for justice to be
    miscarried
When I've known men so long in prison that their babies now are
    married
Hell, I've known men so long in prison they first meet their son out
    on the range
And I don't know that it is justice if we decide you can never
    change

And I don't know that it is justice when there's men inside a cage
And I don't know that it is justice if the scales will never budge
And men in prison with so much legal knowledge they could be a
    judge
And maybe they could have gone in that direction, if they only
    got a nudge
And it's true, I have known men who did a killing for a grudge
But does three seconds of your life make you only human sludge?

And let's not talk about the corporations that profit off it all

Like the predatory phone companies gouging prisoners for a call
Women going broke when her man's conviction's not her fault
I could talk about the scanners and how many hits are false
Families turned away after driving up for hours
Cause I don't know that it is justice when it's so easy to abuse
    powers

I could talk to you for days, and it would all be the same ruin
I know men who did their time out in prison with Assoun
But they'll never be set free to share their voices in these rooms
I know lawyers, guards, and judges who do their best to change
    the tune
But in a society that's broken, that's like reaching for the moon

And I confess, I once believed that every person could be saved
And it took a couple of years and it's true, I got played
I had to face that there's some people who seem to always dig a
    grave
But I still don't believe they deserve solitary just because they
    misbehaved
And I still believe we can do better and we have to find a way
And I'd still rather know I tried even if it means I failed
Because it will never be justice while our solution still is jail

So, from people doing time in Kent down to people in Renous
From people in the county up to people in the SHU
If that was your life story, what do you think you'd do?

SONNET FOR ED

Because I am not one for elegies
Because my nature poems have been burned
Like trees clear cut for penitentiaries
Because I do not hope to turn
Because I have disinfected receivers
And frozen in the Supreme Court lobby
I am, despite myself, still a believer
In justice. Because I have seen your body
In orange I have tried to write verdicts
In poems that would overrule juries
I am, like all of us, not perfect
But I have, with all I have, carried your story
As though it would penetrate the perimeter
My words, for you, and to free all prisoners

৩ 6 ৵

Abolitionist Intimacies

In 2014, the Stockton Police Department in California posted a mug-shot of Jeremy Meeks, a Black man criminalized mostly for gun pos-session. While the intended effect of posting these shots is to stigmatize, the Jeremy Meeks shot elicited a different reaction. The reason? Meeks is "hot." Meeks's "hotness" is itself scripted by social narratives: he is Black but light-skinned, and therefore fits within European conceptions of attractiveness with his "high cheekbones, chiselled face and striking blue eyes" (John 2014). This "hotness" was also framed within heterosexual desires: it was women commentators expressing sexual desire for Meeks who were highlighted in the news stories, as Meeks was named "prison bae" and his photo went viral. Any likely queer male desire was elided, as were any ideas of consent or sexual assault: as writer Laura Donovan observed in an article for *Attn* (2016) about the "prison bae" phenom-enon leading to joking comments about "kidnapping" or "breaking and entering" the subjects of these shots, these comments ignore the realities of prison rape and sexual assault in carceral settings.

Eumi K. Lee (2018) traces the history of publicizing mugshots, argu-ing that in the digital age mugshots are commercialized, capitalizing on the public's voyeuristic fascination with crime and criminals. Lee traces how sites have arisen that post mugshots and charge extortive costs for their removal. Media outlets also benefit from the mugshot industry: in a 2016 survey of seventy-four US newspapers, 40 percent of them pub-lished mugshot galleries (Lee 2018, 570). As Lee observes, the choice of mugshots often reinforces social biases, focusing on "crazy looking" mugshots of people who are addicted or ill, or photos that draw upon racial biases. Law enforcement agencies also joined in, as Lee reports:

> In one of the most egregious examples, the Maricopa County Sheriff's Office, under the leadership of former Sheriff Joe Arpaio, held a daily competition entitled "Mugshot of the Day." Viewers voted American Idol–style for the photograph they

found most appealing. As described by one commentator, "individual humiliation comes as the expense for voyeurism," and these websites capitalize on the public's fascination with these images. (2018, 571)

The practice of posting mugshots is intended to amplify shame and stigma while also pre-supposing guilt, since mugshots are taken before the person has been convicted. Harold Garfinkel described trials as "degradation ceremonies" in 1961; the paradigm of moral indignation, he observes, is public denunciation (421). These rituals further implicate Blackness. In Paul Adjei's (2012) words:

> How do I extricate myself from this Blackness? ... If I am not what I think I am, then who am I? ... How many witnesses can vindicate me? Who can absolve me and proclaim my innocence to these white glancers? It seems, in the white world, everyone is innocent until proven guilty, but being a Black man, I am already guilty until I can prove my innocence. (29)

Black bodies are already "scripted" (Fanon 1968) in the white world, marked as criminal, degenerate, violent, deviant, and already pathologized before they enter the frame.

But I am interested in the reaction to prison bae because of the ways women's sexual desire threatened regimes of stigma and punishment. While posting mugshots for people to laugh at or to bolster narratives of crime is acceptable, women responding by finding the subject desirable threatened the placement of the criminal outside the human. Scolding reactions ensued. Arit John, writing for *The Atlantic*, compared the approval of Meeks's mugshots to the "lovestruck women" who in the cases of Boston marathon bomber Dzhokhar "Jahar" Tsarnaev and Colorado movie-theatre gunman James Holmes were "more focused on their looks than on their crime." John also noted disapprovingly, "The problem is the Stockton PD Facebook page, the epicenter of the meme, also has a memorial dedicated to a fallen officer ... Some people understandably find it upsetting that a jokey meme is getting more attention than a deceased cop" (John 2014, n.p.). Of course, the problem is not a "jokey meme" but that someone labelled deviant, outside the human, should be valued in any way more than a cop; the calculus here is that blue lives matter, and certainly they matter more than the lives of Black accused. Women's desire is here configured as both shallow and pathological by virtue of its proximity to criminality: John chooses two figures considered "beyond the pale" and representative of horror to tie together with the desire for Meeks, thus eliding all accused criminal acts into one conception that defaults to the most extreme accused harms. As Donovan (2016) notes, the many ways men abuse and exploit criminalized women from police rape of sex workers to prison rape is never raised; the harmless desire of women looking at a picture must be condemned, while the actual ways that male power and violence are enacted upon criminalized bodies is completely exited.

The spokesperson for the Stockton PD responded that Meeks was one of the most violent criminals in the area, a charge Meeks denied. Meeks was arrested on five charges of gun possession and one gang charge: both are highly racialized categories of crime. As observed by Howard Sapers (2014) in the Office of the Correctional Investigator report on Canadian prisons, for example, "the label 'gang member' and 'trouble maker' were commonly applied, particularly when three or more Black inmates gathered together (The label 'trouble maker' was also prevalent at the women's institution again when Black women congregated)" (S. 40). In this response, the police attempt to correct the sexual desire for Meeks by asserting his status as criminal and dangerous, as though women who were interested in the mugshot could not already read for themselves the charging information posted along with Meeks's picture. The shame intended to be applied to Meeks by displaying his picture to the public gaze is now applied to the women who blithely ignore the social label of criminal. The attempt by the police to tamp down, redivert, or — failing that — shame those who feel desire is thwarted in this case by women's unapologetic sexuality. Here we see the danger to the constructed systems of punishment from any puncturing of the social discourses that maintain policing and prisons as sites where those deemed "undesirables" are banished.

The response to Meeks's picture raises the question of abolitionist intimacy: the ways in which love, desire, care, longing, touch, and humanity assert themselves against prison walls. These expressions of human relations are dangerous to the prison regime. I was once pulled aside and disciplined in the women's institution where I was teaching creative writing for the offence of "illegally counselling a woman." One of the women had told me she broke up with her girlfriend: I expressed sympathy and said the usual things one says to friends, that it's good to take time for yourself, etc. This was flagged as "counselling" by the guard who overheard the conversation, and since I am not a social worker, it was deemed an inappropriate interest in the woman's life. On other occasions, I was chastised for hugging the women after the writing workshop, for speaking with them about their personal lives shared in their writing, and for suggesting they could continue to contact me once they were released from prison. All of these things — basic forms of human contact and courtesy — were considered violations of the prison policy. I was eventually not permitted to return. Around the same time (or shortly after) I was being chastised for hugging women, one of the male guards was raping women in the institution (CAEFS 2020).

Visitors are also policed for touching; hugging is permitted only at the beginning and at the end of visits. Visitors sit at clear tables where conversation is recorded, and where your hands and body can be surveilled. In particular, young women visiting their boyfriends are policed for any signs of touch. One time in the visiting room of Springhill (a men's federal prison in Nova Scotia), one of the guards overseeing the visits went so far as to announce into the room that a man and his girlfriend were touching, presumably to humiliate her publicly. The guard was a woman; the general response in the room was she was only jealous she could not get some — a response that, while clearly sexist, also demonstrates how this act of sexual shaming backfired. I once received a warning when a young man I was visiting began crying. I reached over to touch his hand in empathy and was promptly summoned to be informed the visit would be ended if I violated the rules again.

In addition to limiting and monitoring physical contact, prisons install dress codes for visitors — largely, again, directed at de-sexualizing young female visitors. The list of restrictions is long: no skirts above the knees, no tight clothing, no sleeveless shirts, nothing see-through. As this is also coupled with prisons' obsession with security, visitors are also banned from wearing shirts with hoods, pockets, any layers, or clothing that is too baggy. One of my friends observed they should probably just sell "visiting tents" to women at the prison doors. Given a warning by a guard about a shirt I was wearing, I informed him that I wore this shirt to work. The response to such challenges to the dress code is commonly "there's rapists in here," as though the clothing women wear, not violent patriarchal power and control, is what causes rape. I speak regularly with other advocates about the ways we are raced and sexed as relatively young Black women advocating with men in prison: because we are also hypersexualized and criminalized as Black women (Collins 2000), we are viewed with the assumption that we must be gang members, bringing in contraband, engaged in sex work, or sexually interested in the prisoners. The notion that male prisoners contact us for legal advocacy or for simple support and care does not fit into this institutional framing where Blackness is always a threat to security and always must be viewed with suspicion and where Black women always embody a deviant sexuality. For Black women who are incarcerated, this extends to accusation of having "attitude" and being disobedient (Sapers 2014) as well as having their bodies policed. A Black woman in Nova Institution informed me she was banned from dancing at prison socials because her body was deemed too provocative (Collins 2000); here, Black female sexuality is both threateningly overt and threateningly queer.

In September of 2017, Halifax newspaper the *Chronicle Herald* published an article with anonymous quotes from a guard at Nova Institution for women objecting to the presence of trans women in the prison (the article no longer exists online). Staff complained, "A female guard could be told to strip-search a male," and "Many (guards) do not want to do this, and they want their rights recognized as much as the inmate's" (Elizabeth Fry Societies of Mainland Nova Scotia and Wellness Within 2017). Nova Institution is now facing a lawsuit by women who were sexually assaulted by a male guard in the prison. As a press release by the Elizabeth Fry Societies of Cape Breton and Mainland Nova Scotia and Wellness Within asserted, "Strip-searching is not a 'right' to be protected" and both organizations acknowledged that "strip searches should be stopped as over 90 percent of women have experienced violence and trauma" (2017, n.p.). Here, we see the legalized sexual assault of prisoners through strip searches reconfigured onto the body of trans women, as though it were the guards who were being violated. The implication is that trans women are reduced to their genitals, which are configured as the site of violence.

In addition to policing bodies, the institution also polices visitors' very response to the guilt of people in prison. For example, to be approved for private family visits (visits in the "trailers" either with family or with spouses or common-law partners), you have to attest to the crime of the person you are visiting. This is, presumably, a liability issue: when you visit, you sign forms indicating you absolve the institution of any harm that might come to you. Making you repeat your understanding of their crime and guilt absolves the institution of further care and responsibility. Should you choose to visit someone with a violent offence, then that is on you. But coupled with all the ways shame is spread in the courtroom (where you sit on the side of the accused, often subject to comments or glares by the crown and, more understandably, the side of the victim); in the questioning by police that family and loved ones are often subjected to; in media commentary; and in broader society, narratives of "women who love murderers" and other pathological framings are common, particularly when it comes to voyeuristic interest in conjugal visits. Women are presented as both infantile and sickening: for example, in the coverage of Paul Bernardo's attempted marriage in 2014, the *National Post* (drawing on a *Toronto Sun* article) breathlessly reported the details of the woman's appearance. "His new paramour — an 'attractive, university-educated' London woman — believes the sinister killer is innocent, the *Sun* said. The thirty-year-old woman even has an ankle tattoo that proclaims she's 'Paul's girl'" (*National Post* 2014, n.p.). The article then goes on to report the comments of her "distraught dad," appealing to patriarchal reason to reassure the reader that now the "vulnerable" woman is reconsidering her attachment.

Anne Laura Stoler (2006) observes that expressions of intimacy are "implicated in the exercise of power" (15). She reviews how colonial states regulated and regulate intimacy, from laws against miscegenation, to intrusions into domestic spaces of social workers, to state-sanctioned rape in war or at carceral sites, to the intimate contact of the captor or torturer: the strip search is an act of abusive intimacy, as is the psychiatric file kept on the prisoner, as is the sympathetic guard, as is the belief that all of this is happening for your own good. Stoler suggests that, for the state, the force of intimacy determines what is "in" or "out," whether through the border, the notion of blood and kin, ranging from religious ecstasy to torture, and opening us to what "haunts ... social relations, to the untoward, to the strangely familiar that proximities and inequalities may reproduce" (14). Stoler urges us to remember that dominance often manifests itself in intimacies: white woman teachers in residential schools understood themselves as loving caregivers for the children, even as they beat the children, separated them from their families, and instilled ideas of racial inferiority (Johnson 2019). Hortense Spillers' (2017) rich discussion of intimacy as "coercive power" for enslaved women is also recognizable within the post-enslavement (or re-enslavement) institution of the prison. In her lecture "Shades of Intimacy: Women in the Time of Revolution" delivered at Barnard College in 2017, Spillers considers the implications for intimacy, love, or touch in the condition of enslavement when families can be separated, when touch was abuse and violation, and where intimate spaces such as the household were places of domination. What can intimacy mean, she asks, if there is no self-ownership? These thoughts expand into the prison context where we can echo the question of what love, care, or contact can mean in an environment of coercion and unfreedom. The "colonizing care" relations of enslavement and imperial occupation, like modern expressions of carceral care through child welfare workers, nurses, and doctors, are simply continued sites of policing (Maynard 2017).

Doctors and nurses work in prisons and collaborate with "security" needs that compromise medical care, such as cutting off medication for "cheeking" pills, standing by when prisoners are brutalized and pepper-sprayed, and participating in cavity searches. In hospitals, nurses and doctors call the police on mentally ill or drug-using patients and for child removals, as in "birth alerts," where social workers flag expectant parents in hospitals so they can be called to remove the child just after its birth. For example, in 2019, Chris Milburn, an emergency room physician in Cape Breton, Nova Scotia, wrote an editorial in the *Chronicle Herald* newspaper in defence of the police charged in the death of Corey Rogers, who asphyxiated on his vomit after being placed into a spit hood and left in the police cells in 2016. Milburn defended the police against the "criminal element," stating among other things that "the amount of ER resources being taken up by criminals has been on the rise," and "anything bad that happens to a criminal now seems to be the fault of the police, and not the individual under arrest" (Milburn 2019, n.p.). He argued for the use of spit hoods, claiming that a "large percentage of patients who would spit on someone trying to help them are carrying dangerous infectious diseases." Characterizing himself as amazed "such a tiny percentage of them do die while in custody," he concluded that "being arrested is the safest thing that could possibly happen to them." Here we see the gaze of medicalized authority (Foucault 1995) where the figure of the doctor uses expertise on criminals in the service of state violence and social control. Care, in this formulation, is reworked into a fear of proximity: the body of the "criminal" is imagined as an always-infectious, always-spitting, always-diseased body that can only be contained and restrained rather than supported or treated. As Sherene Razack (2015) observes in *Dying from Improvement*, the (Indigenous) prisoner-patient is considered to have brought their death on themselves: it is their body's own "vulnerability" that kills them and not the violence of the state through colonization, criminalization, neglect, or active brutality. Such casualties are therefore inevitable, as Milburn (2019) suggests, and we should in fact be "amazed" they do not happen more frequently. In the carceral state, dying is another form of care, and one should be grateful for its agents.

Child welfare workers are able to access the homes of women — largely poor and racialized women — for unannounced visits, searching through fridges and cupboards, demanding information about sexual partners, finances, and mothers' most intimate acts and details (Maynard 2017). Maynard (2017), hooks (1989), and others connect these practices to Black women's work inside white homes, where Black maids and domestics were always under the white gaze.

The strip search, sexual assault by guards, and policing of sexuality are all ways in which the prison intrudes upon and abuses the intimate body space of the criminalized. These are examples of carceral intimacies. Counter to this, I suggest the notion of abolitionist intimacies, characterized by love, care, forgiveness, healing, faith, and uplift in relationships within and outside the prison. My research is based in *friendship* methods of engagement with incarcerated people. Over a decade, I have engaged with incarcerated people and their families, forming relationships, listening, visiting, offering legal support, witnessing, intervening, and loving. I name this method abolitionist intimacy. Intimate work with prisoners is in itself an act of resistance as it defies the notion that prison is a "social death" (Patterson 2018) and that those inside are outside humanity, the public, goodness, etc. Crucial to this research is trust, friendship, keeping my word, meeting needs, and moving beyond either neoliberal system-based interventions (social work, nursing staff, programmers) into everyday caring relationships. Doing this work outside technocratic institutional structures (such as university-funded research, NGOs, government funding) preserves creative and flexible responses to prison oppression (Hesse-Biber and Leavy 2008). In my interactions with prisoners, unlike researchers investigating a single question or temporarily engaging for the purposes of one project, my relationships are ongoing, consistent, and have *no particular research outcome* or goal in mind. Joy, sharing, laughter, kindness, casual discussion, etc. are also central to our interactions.

Abolitionist intimacies are often practised and sustained by women — mothers, girlfriends, support workers, and advocates. These relationships believe in the capacity of the person in prison for love, for return, for change. Visiting rooms are largely full of women visitors, often impoverished (Hanington 2020) who sacrifice to place money on phones, drive hours to prisons, pay for prison boxes, and remind the incarcerated person there is a home to return to. Prison traumatizes families, creates economic harm, and victimizes children as "secondary victims of crime" (Cunningham and Baker 2004, 2) who may experience depression, disruptions to education, grief, and shame from having an incarcerated parent. Often these relationships are stigmatized: mothers are seen as insufficiently critical of their children, girlfriends are seen as having low self-esteem, and children are seen as damaged or as future criminals marked by the prison space.

Visiting men is not frequently placed into a feminist frame but is more likely seen as a sign only of women's acceptance of male bad behaviour. In women's prisons, visiting rooms are comparatively empty. Meghan MacEachern's (2019) study of incarcerated women in New Brunswick (a provincial setting) describes how women "displayed mixed feelings about access to their children, visitations with their children, and experiencing social supports relating to their children. A common sentiment was the coldness of viewing the children behind bars, and this led many to not want to have their children/family view them in that light at all" (119). As MacEachern observes, "Considering this example in light of penal governance, keeping the women from having visits free of contact restrictions such as glass windows is a way to maintain control, carefully disguised under the umbrella of safety" (120). Even in federal, where contact visits are allowed, women may prefer to spare their children the trauma of visiting. In a 2013 report on self-injury, the Office of the Correctional Investigator found that the majority of women self-harming were Indigenous, and most of these women had no history of any prison visits. For example, one woman had not had a visitor in thirteen years and another has not had a visitor in six years. Two of the women had a few occasional visits — one woman had five visits over a six-year period and the other had one visitor over the course of 2011. (Office of the Correctional Investigator 2013, S. 19)

It is important to acknowledge this gender dynamic: in a patriarchal, white supremacist society, men will be privileged over women, and women — who are double offenders both as criminals and then again as bad women (Faith 2011) trespassing the expected gender norms of womanhood — are abandoned and exited from society. Men in prison receive care from family in ways women in prison may not, and as primary caregivers, women also face the added punishment of child welfare involvement (MacEachern 2019; Hanington 2020) and loss of their children. For Indigenous women in particular, the child welfare–prison cycle reflects the multi-generational trauma, social control, and assimilation visited upon Indigenous women and families through colonialism (Hanington 2020, 38).

While visiting can reinforce gender roles and patterns, acts of love in a prison setting also hold the potential for challenge to prison's totalizing regime. Idil Abdillahi has described intimate prison relationships as potentially queer (No Life Left Behind, Episode 1). Viewed outside the lens of heteronormative relationships, sexual relationships in prison, in all their iterations, offer a challenge to state-sanctioned, white, hetero, middle-class, cis-normative constructions of respectable and therefore acceptable sexualities. As Sarah Lamble (2015) notes, "Queer, trans, and gender non-conforming people, particularly those from low-income backgrounds and communities of colour, are directly targeted by criminalization, punishment, and imprisonment" (289). Queer relationships are thus already present in prisons, and are often monitored, punished, or surveilled. Women in Nova Institution, for example, informed me of the reluctance of prison authorities to support women seeking to marry their partners inside prison. Trans men were frequently held in the maximum-security unit; these assessments of risk cannot be separated from transphobic constructions of danger and sexual assault. Under state control, the state also intervenes into intimate relationships, up to and including one's relationship with one's own body: male prisoners, for example, can be charged for masturbation (Hughes 2020). In 2013, Quebec prisoner Haris Naraine complained after officials in Archambault Institution cancelled two porn channels, arguing the prisoners paid for the channels, but CSC ordered all x-rated channels cut (CBC 2015, n.p.). Naraine argued that Corrections was infringing on the prisoners' freedom of expression rights and had no right to censor what prisoners legally bought.

Private family visits are framed in heteronormative ways that privilege state-sanctioned family structures: family, for example, is defined largely in terms of the nuclear family, although more recent adjustments do at least superficially acknowledge Indigenous notions of kinship (CSC 2016). For non-family members, the criteria demand an "enduring bond of friendship and trust" where "both individuals shared significant life experiences" and where "one of the individuals contributed significantly to the moral or spiritual development of the other" (CSC 2016, Annex A under Definitions, "close personal relationship"). This explicit moral framing both privileges length of time as a measure of the strength and authenticity of relationships and also introduces subjective moral framings: Does a queer relationship formed during homelessness or a relationship between drug users qualify as contributing to moral development? What about friendships on the frontlines of political resistance? These attempts to police intimacy once again elevate the state authority as the arbiter of appropriate care, affection, love, and pleasure.

"It seems clear," writes Hortense Spillers, that

> "family" as we practice and understand it "in the West" — the *vertical* transfer of a bloodline, of a patronymic, of titles and entitlements, of real estate and the prerogatives of "cold cash," from *fathers* to *sons* and in the supposedly free exchange of affectional ties between a male and a female of *his* choice — becomes the becomes the mythically revered privilege of a free and freed community. (1987, 74)

The assertion of "family" in a prison space can be separated from raced notions of neither family nor motherhood. White parents frequently report to me that prison officials have informed them their son does not belong in there; the implication is their son is not like those others, those Black people, whose natural habitat is the prison. In the pathologized reading of Black woman/motherhood, visiting the prison is our natural state, the culmination of our at-once dominating and neglectful parenting practices. For Black women, our love and care have always been twisted: we have always, in a so-called post-enslavement world, been read as preparing our children for future incarceration. The prison in this sense "fathers" Black men and can offer "the help they need," unlike the imagined absent fathers of their own community. The prison as white authority figure properly disciplines unruly Black men/children. To assert our own care in these spaces, to illicitly touch the hand, to send expensive clothing so our Black men can look and feel good inside, to drop everything for the phone call — these are "insurgent" acts, to use Spillers' claiming of "insurgent ground" (1987, 80): a "connectedness" that is "different from the moves of a dominant symbolic order, pledged to maintain the supremacy of race" (75). I want to remove these acts solely from the phrase of the nurturing, to politicize them as abolitionist acts that defy the prison. As Butch Lee (2000) observes about Harriet Tubman:

> To trivialize Harriet Tubman the capitalist patriarchy pictures her as an idealized woman by their definition, who makes a life of helping others. Thus her deeds are squeezed into women's assigned maternal role as nurturer, helper and rescuer of men (who then go on to do the important things). But Harriet wasn't repping Mother Teresa. (5)

Prisons rely upon the investment of family in its structures and policies. Without family to place money on phones, removing those privileges through segregation practices, for example, would be less of a punishment. Canteen, visits, contact are all necessary to the prison in controlling prisoners as fights are more likely to break out without these things, and prisoners with something to lose are more likely to behave docilely. Linda Mussell identifies how CSC uses family as a "rehabilitation tool" where families are imagined as properly collaborating in managing criminalized people (Wellness Within conference 2020). The family here is seen as an extension of state control and normative structures. Brenda Cossman (2002) argues that under neoliberalism, economic responsibilities are privatized. Social responsibility for care is shifted from a collective social duty to the private family sphere; to expand this reading, families under state punishment regimes take on the responsibility for both causing and fixing crime, shifting the focus away from the role of unequal social structures in criminalization on one hand and social supports such as housing or treatment on the other hand.

Many feminist commentators have argued that notions of family under colonial capitalism reinforce social dominance structures, reproductive control, and gender inequality. Sharon McIvor (2004) shows how marriage imposed colonial and patriarchal norms on Indigenous communities, particularly harming and dispossessing Indigenous women's power and knowledge. Hazel Carby (1997) points out,

> Three concepts which are central to feminist theory become problematic in their application to Black women's lives: "the family," "patriarchy," and "reproduction." When used they are placed in a context of the herstory of white (frequently middle-class) women and become contradictory when applied to the lives and experiences of Black women. (46)

Even more disturbingly, with the rise of electronic surveillance technologies, family and community become prisons where the carceral gaze is extended into the domestic space. For criminalized communities, electronic surveillance turns Black and Indigenous homes into panopticons.

While there is no way for our interactions with prison to not be problematized in some way, abolition cannot depend upon cutting off the prisoner to spite the prison face. In other words, we cannot decide not to interact with prison because that would mean not interacting with people in prison, so we must resist in other ways and in spite of the carceral structure. As Carby identifies, the "Black family has functioned as a prime source of resistance to oppression" (1997, 46). Removing visiting from the "proper" gendered frame and placing it in a feminist "insurgent" (Spillers 1987) one allows us to understand how our acts of care are also acts of organization, acts of rebellion, acts of strengthening, and acts that prepare our loved ones for liberation. They are also often accompanied by subversive acts: the three-way call; the surreptitious picture taken by a phone hidden in a baby's stroller; changing the value of the boxes sent in so people receive more expensive goods than allowed; sustaining the network of texting and calling and updates that develop between the loved ones of prisoners on the outside (sending a text for another prisoner who can't call, for example); and having conversations that, even while monitored, condemn and call out the prison conditions and authorities. "Keep your head up," we say, meaning even if you are keeping your head down and just getting through, know that you still have pride and being; make it through; come home to us. Prison is not forever. Our abolition begins even in its small, seemingly powerless ways.

During the COVID-19 pandemic, Jerry, who like many older prisoners lives with compromised immunity and other health problems from premature aging in prison (Iftene 2019), told me if there was an outbreak in his prison, he had stockpiled enough food to simply stay in his cell alone for two weeks while he prayed not to die. Because Canada did not undertake a program of releases of federal prisoners during COVID-19, Jerry's only strategy for survival was to isolate himself from human contact. This matched the institutional response of securitizing prisons in response to the pandemic: creating lockdown quarantine ranges, ending visits and programs, and limiting time out of cell. As on the streets, prisons chose to "police their way out of a pandemic" (McClelland and Luscombe 2020), a practice which re-targeted people who are Black, Indigenous, migrant, queer and trans, drug users, experiencing poverty and other already criminalized populations (Dryden 2020). Prisons already structure themselves to interrupt solidarities between prisoners — for example, by dividing populations into general population and protected custody ostensibly for security and safety reasons — but also as a tool to reduce co-operation and common cause across prison populations. In the Burnside prison strike of 2018, the manifesto written by the prisoners began by locating itself in these solidarities across populations, between people inside prison and on the outside, and even with the workers in the jail:

We, the prisoners of Burnside, have united to fight for change. We are unified across the population in non-violent, peaceful protest.

We are calling for support from the outside in solidarity with us. We believe that it is only through collective action that change will be made.

We recognize that the staff in the jail are workers who are also facing injustice. We are asking for a more productive rehabilitative environment that supports the wellbeing of everyone in the system. These policy changes will also benefit the workers in the jail. (Jones 2018)

Absent a response from prison authorities that recognized that public health measures would be served by housing prisoners in community — that prison is always a health risk and can never be safe — Jerry recognized he was forced into a position where contact with other prisoners could threaten his health. He also recognized that the guards would spread the infection in the prison, as they are the ones moving back and forth between the prison and community, moving between ranges, and entering cells for inspection. But as he could not evade their authority, the only solution was to cut himself off from those he was incarcerated with. Due to the jail's inaction, any intimacy between incarcerated people became viewed as a potential site of transfer, where breath, touch, and shared food could all be a death sentence. In the midst of all this, prisons continued to function as ongoing sites of death where prisoners are beaten and pepper-sprayed; where they die by suicide, die by medical neglect, die by suffocation, die by guards kneeling on them, die by colonization, and die by racism. Instead of confronting the deadliness of prison as an institution, corrections officials pretend death is an unusual state, one sited in the prisoners and one that can be controlled through more securitization rather through health measures and medical care. Sickness and death are the constant condition of the prison, not a new crisis: the pandemic is punishment, colonization, and racism.

To insist on loving, desiring, caring for, or being in relationship with someone in prison is to push back against not only state narratives but the very real mechanisms that stifle humanity, goodness, the possibility of transformation, or transcending the category of criminal. Segregation, lockdowns, high security ratings, recorded phone calls, and monitored visits all either remove or attempt to mediate contact with the outside world. Every visitor in a federal prison is subjected to a drug scan and then sniffed by a dog as a follow up; body scanners are now installed inside prisons and jails to image prisoners as they move from range to range or to the outside world. Visitors attending family or conjugal visits have their belongings searched, including items such as psychiatric medication, lube, and birth control pills, for example, which reveal personal details of their lives to the prison officials. Every phone call from a Nova Scotia provincial prison on the Telmate system begins with informing you, "This call is subject to recording and monitoring." These sophisticated monitoring systems scan calls for evidence of three-ways, coded words, and other contraband conversations, as well as potentially providing calls as evidence to prosecutors or police. And given that these systems are located in the United States, this means the voices, information, and data of Canadians are being surveilled across borders. As Simone Browne (2015) observes about biometric technologies such as facial recognition, computer webcams, and touchless faucets, the application of these technologies is in the "verification, identification, and automation practices that enable the body to function as evidence" (109). Connecting these technologies to the historical practices of branding as a surveillance and identifying practice, Browne links modern surveillance techniques to the "commodification of Blackness":

> When we think of our contemporary moment when "suspect" citizens, trusted travellers, prisoners, welfare recipients and others are having their bodies informationalized by way of biometric surveillance, sometimes voluntarily and sometimes without consent or awareness, and then stored in large-scale automated databases, some managed by the state, and some owned by private interests, we can find histories of these accountings of the body in, for example, the inventory that is the *Book of Negroes*, slave ship manifests that served maritime insurance purposes, banks that issued insurance policies to slave owners against the loss of enslaved labourers, and branding as a technology of tracking Blackness that sought to make certain bodies legible as property. (2015, 128)

Against these inhuman, dehumanizing violations of person and privacy, abolitionist intimacy in face-to-face, voice-to-voice, or hand-to-hand refusals of separation realize a world that is still human, one where prisoners are not left behind. In bell hooks' phrase, this intimacy is an "act of resistance, a political gesture that challenges the politics of domination" (1989, 8).

"We Gon Be Alright"

On Activism, Death, and Survival

This essay was first published in the Halifax Examiner *on March 23, 2019.*

We've been talking a lot about our deaths lately.

If I die before you, I instruct the people I love, don't let my name be used for wack shit. I'm counting on you. I follow with instructions for various scenarios. If I die violently, remember how I felt about prisons. Don't let one of the racist crowns take my case. Don't let people water my politics down at my funeral. Don't let me be at some funeral with police if I die in some kind of mass attack. Don't let the people who had no use for me in life use me in death. Don't let people pretend I was a saint that I wasn't. Don't let people take in death what I wouldn't give them in life. Don't. Don't. Don't.

I'm not imagining my death; I'm just protective of it. Perhaps that's because it seems Blackness can't be uncoupled from dying. The Afro-pessimists argue this, that to be Black is to be haunted by captivity, violence, and death. I had a friend once who, when people asked her how it was going, would always respond, "I'm alive. And that means something because we're not supposed to be here."

Perhaps it's just that historical sense, the way our Black grandmothers worked all their lives to only be lauded in death. The funeral is the most expressive space they had. It was a resistant act, this way of dying, the way our enslaved ancestors sung about stealing away home and they meant death and they meant liberation and they meant escape. When we died, we believed our souls would return to Africa. We believed we would walk again in our homelands. Our body could no longer be used for labour. It was our final triumph.

It's like how a young man in prison once paused and said to me thoughtfully, Well, one way or another, we all will be released.

But there are more practical reasons for thinking about our deaths too. We can't pretend this work doesn't take a toll.

Idil says to me what we never talk about: Somebody has to clean up the blood. Even to each other, we don't talk about the hardest, most traumatic parts of this work. Who planned the funeral after the shooting. Who mopped out the apartment. And who can't speak about it while those names become currency for activism. Who isn't filling their resume with that work, and who is eating off it.

People talk about self-care, but what can that mean when the people who care most deeply for you, and the ones who you love in return, are the people to whom you owe your labour? It isn't a burden to do this work, not when the trust and solidarity and profound love you build by your commitment to each other are the reward. But still, when the calls from segregation come in the evenings, it means there's no going to movies, or out to dinner, or even watching a whole show on Netflix. And that's the work that won't get a tenured job. That's the work that puts pain in your body and takes years off your life.

But when M. calls me and tells me I sound down, and I tell him I don't know if I'll have a job next year, he says, I get a welfare cheque every month. Let me send you that. Someone like you should never have to ask for help.

Nobody else — not the heads of departments, not the colleagues and friends — nobody else has offered everything they have like that. This is why we answer the phone evening after evening.

But still, sometimes love is a ragged blanket to warm yourself with at night.

I think often about Rocky's portrait in the law school at Dalhousie. I knew Rocky, knew at the end of his life he was still having to scramble for cash. The institutions that spend tens of millions on buildings could have funded a Chair for Rocky Jones. If they had wanted to, if they valued him, they could have done it. After all the years of fighting white supremacy until his heart literally gave out inside him, the institutions to which he gave so much could have made a place for him to live out his life in dignity. They chose not to. And the same universities that couldn't spend a few thousand to make sure Rocky was taken care of display his picture, now he is safely dead.

Desmond says to me, we may not be religious, but what we do is like a religious act. We imagine and work toward a better world. But the heaven we are trying to make is here on Earth. And while we are living here and struggling, we are in hell. But heaven and hell are the same place for us. So, every day we wake up in hell, and we have to do our best to enter heaven. Every single day, we have to try to knock on heaven's door. We have to sacrifice for that. And we have to pay the price for that.

We don't hold anything back in this work. Not savings, not our tongues that get us labelled troublemakers, not even our tears, although we push them back and get up the next morning and keep fighting on. Because someone has to buy the groceries, put the clothes in the prison boxes, pay the gas for visits. Somebody has to hold the hands in court and call the lawyer and visit the jail and take the call from the suicide cell.

And somebody has to stand up at the meetings, and in the places of power, and at the panels, and even the parties to call relentlessly on those with the power to do more, to end it. And when you stand in that love, and solidarity, and rage, you can't expect to have the bills paid. You can't expect to have the comfort of the world too. You have to make your choices.

Sometimes I lie in bed and think about the books I should have written, the papers I could have published, the poems and articles and chapters I didn't give my time to. And everyone tells me I wouldn't be lying here if I had just written those things. But then I ask myself, which life would I exchange for that book? Whose life was worth less than a chapter? And I know I wouldn't choose differently, just as nobody would choose differently, not if you knew the life that was in front of you, that you had the power to sustain and hold.

We are the living archive, I remind myself, and there is no tenured position, no degree, no qualification, that can give me what is worth more than one life.

I make plans for leaving sometimes. I imagine other cities, cities where I pretend people would open doors for me, and where I wouldn't have to worry year to year about whether I'll have somewhere to live. But then I ask myself if I can walk away from the lives that offer me their last penny, the ones who pass the phone around on the ranges believing I will know how to fix things and so I figure out what to do, because when people trust you like that there is nothing, nothing you won't do to pay that back.

It is not that I save them; it is that their trust and care sustains and nurtures me, that every day when I despair, when I don't know how I can pick up and rebuild again, when I don't know how I can fight these fights without sickening and dying from it, it is their voices that remind me, over and over, who I am and why we do this work.

And these are my instructions to the people around me. If I die before you, make sure those who loved me and whom I loved are the people at my funeral. Scatter my ashes outside the prisons of this province so I can haunt them forever. Don't use my name for wack shit, and don't let the institutions that wouldn't love me in life take hold of me in death. If I die violently, remember that I hated prisons and honour me.

I'm not imagining my death; these are my expressions of my commitment to the living. To my life and the life of others. To the sacrifice that isn't a sacrifice, but a sacrament, a blessing.

EASTER SUNDAY, 2018
For Randy Riley, wrongfully convicted.

I am in a slowly dying community

It is Easter Sunday
A year since your mother died
After the first week of your trial

And we are in good spirits

I should make duck, your aunt says
And one of your uncles disagrees
Duck is too greasy, he says
And pauses
Especially the black ducks

And across the table your other uncle says
Have you ever seen a black duck?
And then he ducks

You sent me here
My family would love to have you
You tell me
When you find out I have no plans for Easter
No one should be alone on Easter
You say
Before the cell door closes on you

And you
Thinking of me, send me
To the love of your family
And jokes about white folk
And laughter

On Tuesday we will squeeze our Blackness into hard courtroom
    benches
Try to control the black looks on our faces
Discipline our unruly Black hands and the twists of our lips

The tucks of our tongues
And the volume of our voices

For the white gaze
Of juries
And crowns
And media

On Tuesday we will be criminals
And family of criminals

But today
On Easter
There is storytelling
And joyous loudness
And Blackness freed

And pie to take home

We remember

We are still here
There is good in us
This is how we survive

MANY OF MY BROTHERS

Many of my brothers gone away in a box
So many many lives are measured out in ticking clocks
All our Black fingers are sore from picking locks
While the rich all invest in rising prison stocks
And the rich all invest in those taser stocks
Young Black man dead on the street from electrical shocks
Same company makes the body cameras they sell to cops
When they make a killing, we pay the cost

Our police force purchased a tank for a rapid response
Infiltrate our communities with agents and ops
There's cameras on the corner of the vacant lot
No grocery store, but there's a place that grooms dogs
No school anymore, but the donuts are hot
Count yourself lucky if you have a sidewalk
Only real estate you call your own is your grave plot
Stole the deed to your land while your grandmother sobs

No subsidized daycare for the tots
Mould and rot in the housing like you live in a squat
Government can't invest money in shelter cots
But they offered a tax break to Amazon
Soon they'll give your job to a white robot
Criminal record check so your resumes dropped
No amnesty for Black folks when they legalized pot
Trudeau said he smoked but he never got caught
Now we've got four times the cannabis arrests in the Wortley
    Report
One third of Black men with a charge in court

Systemic racism so you can't get a shot
Human rights complaints against fire, transit, and cops
Working at Leon's, noose tied in a knot
Shopping at Sobeys, cashier is calling her boss
It looks like you on the tape, you're that blurry blot
North Preston address so your resume's gone
Sounds like a Black name so it doesn't belong

Restaurant fired you for natural hair done up in locs
No security clearance to work on the docks
No options but guns, hustling, or rocks

Half of the jail just needs detox
Most of the rest just need a therapist or someone to talk
Childhood trauma that goes unresolved
What you get is a tray pushed through a slot
All you get is some prayers and hand it over to God

They say it's just Trump, they say it's just Fox
They say the rhetoric's contagious like chicken pox
As if brown and Black bodies aren't lining their pockets
As if Indigenous and Black people don't make up our docket
As if the landfills and dumps ain't got our community toxic
As if Canada's ever welcomed you if your skin is like chocolate
As if we aren't here at the bottom, making their profit

Live-in nanny from Jamaica watching their child 'round the clock
Blueberry-picking, modern-day slave crops
They did a poll if too many immigrants go to a mosque
Are there too many immigrants not of old Canadian stock?
They call you illegal once there's a border you cross
Crammed into container ships and trucks like livestock
Kids in a cage made the world pretend that they're shocked
But indefinite immigration detention is something we've got
Tents at the border, Haitians without the Red Cross
Black man in snow to his chest with his fingers lost
Like those starlight tours in the cold and the frost

We're worth more to them dead, we're worth more to them
    dropped
We're worth more in a cell and a prison shop
Two dollars a day in those prison jobs
Got them dishing out food or pushing a mop
An American company profits when you call your mom or your
    pops
Paid lawyer's got a suit from Hugo Boss
If you don't teach them to read, then they'll be in the dock

While those small towns get prisons to replace the fish and the
   logs
The correctional college is opening a record number of spots
Just like back in the day they auctioned us off
Just like back in the day they chased us down with the dogs
Just like back in the day they built our community on rocks

They say earn your way out the hood like the rappers and jocks
They only give you a mural if you get shot
Got us trapped on the streets in the school of hard knocks
They're preparing the outline of our bodies in chalk
They say they won't apologize for police stops
They're consulting with Black folk like we're just their props
We can't breathe because they follow us when we walk
Security guards stalking our mothers in shops
Say slavery's over like we ever forgot
When we're still at the bottom and they're at the top

This colonial province named for New Scots
School-to-prison pipeline connecting the dots
Life sentence got you buried under the prison block

Coups around the world, drones that always drop
Bombing campaigns from Israel to Iraq
Global white supremacy never, ever stops
Prison industrial complex always on the clock
Black life on a timer, tick tick tock
Too many of my brothers gone away in a box

∽ 7 ∾

Black Feminist Teachers

In *Barracoon: The Story of the Last "Black Cargo"* (2018), Zora Neale Hurston grapples with the notion of voice and silencing. Throughout the book, Hurston tries to work out, in the form of her telling, how to represent the story of Kossula, the last living survivor of the African slave trade. Hurston rejects traditional anthropological stances of authority and objectivity, instead writing Kossula's story in his own voice. But Hurston also recognizes her own presence in the text as teller, transcriber, and witness; the text also contends with how she represents her own voice in relationship to Kossula's.

In the introduction, Hurston identifies who has had the power to tell the narrative of the slave trade:

> All these words from the seller, but not one word from the sold. The Kings and Captains whose words moved ships. But not one word from the cargo. The thoughts of the "black ivory" and "the coin of Africa" had no market value. Africa's ambassadors to the New World have come and worked and died, and left their spoor, but no recorded thought. (2018, eBook)

Hurston here recognizes how power structures narrative: in conversation with Kossula, Hurston confronts not only how to unsilence the lives of Black people but also how the forms of her own telling must shape themselves to Kossula's story. As Genevieve Sexton (2003) describes,

> An analysis of Hurston's textual, structural and narrative framing reveals a tension between the desire to hear and understand the urgent heart of the testimony, and the rejection engendered because of the inability to compensate for the loss, violence, or injustice that the testimony is intended to mitigate. *Barracoon* thus shows a conflict between looking to testimony in order

to access the atrocity of the past as a means of recovering this rupture, and the simultaneous recognition that the past is interminably closed off as inaccessible and intangible. Kossula's testimony — the testimony of the last witness — therefore speaks at a precipice of loss. (191)

In her first meeting with Kossula, Hurston describes entering through a "wide open" door and an unlocked gate, signifying that Kossula is at home. Hurston calls him by his African name, which immediately engenders recognition from Kossula: "Oh Lor', I know it you call my name. Nobody don't callee me my name from cross de water but you. You always callee me Kossula, jus' lak I in de Affica soil!" (2018, eBook). Throughout the book, as she gives place to Kossula's voice, Hurston repeatedly narrates her returns: the gifts she brings, the conditions when she arrives, whether Kossula has company, her method of transport. She worries that he will not want to receive her, that he will grow tired of their visits: she is conscious of her position as interloper and the disruption of seeking his narrative. In this, Hurston refuses the position in the text of authoritative seer. By highlighting her own comings and goings into Kossula's life, and thus into the text, she provides a model for thinking through how we ethically tell the stories of horror and Black pain as we seek to bear witness. In returning to the open door anew, in highlighting her arrivals, Hurston signposts her own interventions into the text, a heralding of her stepping back as narrator as she seeks to reproduce Kossula's voice. In foregrounding her stepping into and out of the text — arriving to hear Kossula's story but allowing the storytelling itself to unfold in his own voice as represented by Hurston — Hurston grapples with not only how to tell Kossula's tale but also how to resist or refuse a tradition of anthropological narrative where the white male voice assumes domination.

I think of Hurston's attempts to step through Kossula's door, to engage in his language, to forge space of recognition, in relation to my own attempts at telling. Attending the Fall Writers Retreat at the Banff Centre, where I wrote the first draft of parts of this book, I realized something during one of the reading nights where the writers share their work: in contrast to other writers, I never describe people visually. Instead, I begin so often in conversation, in orality. In my tellings, people are known by what we have spoken of. This is not surprising when so often the accounts of state violence I share begin with phone conversations, a reflection of the hidden and inaccessible places that are prisons, shelters, institutions, places of detention. I came to see my writing as being about the telling of these relationships. In *The Culture of Punishment* (2009), Michelle Brown discusses the "penal spectator" to capture both individual and institutional practices of looking at others' pain from a distance, in the process perpetuating ideologies of punishment. She suggests that this distancing of pain and the spectacle of suffering authors carcerality. Hurston's careful deconstructing of her own looking through the image of the open gate reminds us of this gaze and attempts to reduce the distancing that comes with the narration of suffering.

As I am writing this, the mother of an incarcerated Black woman calls me. I had talked to this woman's father but had not understood what was being asked of me. I thought the family was looking for legal assistance, and so I directed them to the Elizabeth Fry Society, then followed up with the workers there to ensure they made contact. But it was not services they wanted. On the phone, her mother tells me her daughter writes. She saw my name in an email about a panel on writing, and this was a sign to her that she needed to reach out. "I'm trying to save my daughter's life," she tells me. "I'm calling you as a Black woman." What she wanted was not legal services, or social work, or information about community living. She wanted a Black woman to simply listen to her daughter, to take her calls, and to support her. It was not help with the system she needed but the healing work Black women have done with each other as survival for generations: someone who wouldn't shame her daughter, who would understand her, and who would make time. What she was calling for and upon is a Black feminist praxis of shared experience.

I Say It Was the Women

The Fight for Abdilahi Elmi

> It was the women who restored us.
> — Eric M. Roach, "I Say It Was the Women"

By the time we hear about Abdilahi Elmi's deportation, it is almost too late. The first time Dunia emailed me, a month before we made contact, I didn't get her message. Dalhousie University cut off my email a couple of months before, and I can no longer use that mailbox.

Hannah Arendt talks about the banality of evil. And then there is the banality of bureaucracy. Elmi's life could turn on the length of time Dalhousie allows our mailboxes to be maintained. Not even a decision, just a password expiring.

∽ ∾

Elmi is scheduled for deportation on August 26, 2019. We have less than a month to stop it. The people in Edmonton know about our work with Abdoul Abdi, so they reach out. Like Abdoul, Elmi is a child refugee from Somalia. Like Abdoul, he was taken from his mother, taken into foster care, left to the streets. When we were fighting Abdoul's case, we knew there were so many other people in the same circumstances. Still, to be here a year after Abdoul's deportation was stopped, fighting the same thing, is dispiriting. When I tell Abdoul's sister Fatuma, she says, I thought they changed the law. I thought what happened to my brother would never happen to anyone else.

The people in Edmonton have been fighting for Elmi for over a year. This is the work that never hits the headlines. Dunia Nur is a young Somali Canadian diaspora woman. She founded the African Canadian Civic Engagement Council. They take youth in the community and teach them about medicine, about law, about social work. When young people can't get education, they create tailored programs for them. They care for the young men seen as unsalvageable, unlovable, deportable. They bring life.

Dunia's been taking Elmi's calls from jail every day. When he was out in community, in rehab, she drove him around, bought bus tickets, advocated for him with the workers. She has given her life over to supporting him. Moréniké Ọláòṣebìkan and Emmanuel Onah, both young Nigerian-descended people, are there fighting too.

For over a year, they have been going to politicians, being promised their representatives will help Elmi. The community has gathered money they don't have, giving it to lawyers charging fees they know will be paid in an emergency.

When we fought for Abdoul, we didn't take a single private meeting. When politicians started feeling embarrassed, they offered, but we turned it down. They always want to get us behind closed doors where we can't be seen. These deportations are done in hidden ways, so we want everything to be out in public. We tell the Edmonton advocates, Stop meeting. There's an election on. Crash their events. Follow them around with banners. Get up and ask them questions. We learned these things with our bodies, getting up over and over when people wanted us to stop. Now we pass these lessons on.

But, time. With Abdoul we had more time. Here, the clock is ticking. We make a WhatsApp group and Dunia changes the name every day, counting down the days until the deportation is scheduled.

People in prison talk to me about time, how it means different things in captivity than it does in the free world. They talk about how time sits on you, how you try to do your own time, how you wait for time, fill time, are controlled by time. So often, I'm dealing with too much time. Now, we don't know if we have enough.

Desmond says to me, Are we really doing this again? We both pause and then start laughing, incredulous at ourselves, at this system which grinds up Black bodies over and over. Fuck our plans, our deadlines, our lives. We're doing this again.

Desmond is co-ordinating with the Somali mothers in Toronto. He met them at a police board meeting. The mothers were presenting on initiatives for their community, and Desmond was there for Dafonte Miller, a young Black man beaten by an off-duty police officer and his brother. Dafonte lost his eye. Or rather, his eye was taken. Desmond's group sits through the presentation by the mothers, and then they disrupt the meeting. The mothers join them in solidarity. Later, the police board tries to say the group demanding justice for Dafonte disrespected and interrupted the mothers. These mothers are the ones who join the campaign in Toronto. As if the police could ever divide us.

Dunia tells me later the only thing she remembers from all of this is the feeling of panic, every minute, every day.

And God, Black women are so amazing. Here you are, Fatuma, fighting again for everyone except yourself. Our great-great-grandmothers who tended bare provision grounds, spelling meals with cracked hands. Here you are, Dunia, as though the world turns upon your love. Here you are, Somali mothers. We have a miscommunication about the time of an action in the office of the local MP in Edmonton, and so the mothers burst in all day, in groups of one or two or four, yelling "Free Elmi!" before they rush out. They are wearing red hijabs for Elmi, like Superman's cape, lifting the world with one hand.

Maybe they won't get the papers in time, I say optimistically. If Elmi doesn't have travel documents to Somalia, they can't send him. It means he'll be sitting in jail, like so many other deportees are being held indefinitely year after year, but at least it might buy us some extra weeks or months.

But it turns out Canada is expediting papers for Somalis through Washington, DC. If we get to August 26 and we haven't managed to stay the deportation, he'll be on the plane.

Oh, how hollow their outrage about Trump and kids in cages. When there's a Black body to be rid of, let nothing stand in the way.

Elmi writes a letter to Dunia. At the end, he writes:

God bless you and I will always remember you no matter where I'm at. It's hard to see people that care in the community but you proved me wrong, you are good at your work and what you do, remember that when hard times come your way. I really appreciate everybody that helped me. Tell them I said thank you to every one of them and don't think I forgot about Emmanuel. He is a good man tell him he will always be my friend. Tell him if he wants to beat me in chess to come to Somalia and I will beat him in chess. I will miss you guys. Nothin' but love. I'm happy that I met you and him.

PS I hope you love the picture that I coloured for you.

He is already planning for the day he is gone.

౼ ౼

Cruelty may not be banal, but it is casual. The border agents come to Elmi and he tells them he's scared to go to Somalia. He doesn't know how to survive. They ask him what he would need to survive, and he says he doesn't know, he guesses maybe $500. Elmi does not have a lawyer. He struggles to read, although he composes poetry and rap. He is alone and incarcerated. They tell him they'll give him $500. Later, in court, they say the issue of whether Somalia is too dangerous to deport him to is moot, because he asked for money and got it.

Before he was apprehended by Canadian Border Services and put into Edmonton remand, Elmi was in a program at the Salvation Army. One night, after a difficult family encounter, he relapsed. Elmi has been addicted since he was sixteen. Dunia is working with him to teach him his culture, to return him to himself, but it doesn't happen overnight. The workers at the Salvation Army call the police on Elmi. Dunia runs down there, argues with them and begs them, but they take him away anyway.

Where is the salvation in that?

౼ ౼

Morénike is getting married in a couple of weeks. We message with her while she's planning her wedding. Desmond is finishing his book. He spends a weekend camping, takes calls by the river. Robyn Maynard is rushing through airports. Syed Hussan from the Migrant Rights

Network is supposed to be on vacation. I am in Jamaica. Desmond and I plan two press conferences while I'm sitting by the pool. I write the text for people to send to MPs in the back of a car headed up Blue Mountain. It's supposed to be summer.

Ben Perryman, Abdoul's lawyer, sends me an email. He tells me Audrey Macklin, a professor in human rights law at the University of Toronto, heard about Elmi's case from reading Robyn Maynard's article in the *Toronto Star* calling to stop the deportation. Audrey began cold-calling every lawyer she knew who might know about the case until she reached Ben. Ben is on vacation too, but I keep texting him anyway, and he keeps offering help. Ben knows what to do. He connects us to Audrey. The only option we have left is to appeal to the United Nations Human Rights Committee. The clinic started a petition for Abdoul, but then we won in court. We need it now. Vincent Wong stays up almost twenty-four hours straight and gets the application to them. Now we wait.

Dunia connects Elmi to me. His voice is tinny, far away on a bad jail line. He thanks me over and over and I haven't done anything yet. This gratefulness, it flows all the time in this work. Thank you for taking the call. I don't want to bother you, I know you're busy, they say. And I say, it's nothing, it's nothing, but when we give people nothing, this little feels like plenty.

The Hoyo Collective is a Somali mother's collective in Edmonton. Dunia records voice messages for me, speaking to me of the mothers in two-minute fragments.

Dunia says, What I would like to share with you today is why these mothers decided to put their money, time, car, gas, everything they had they gave it to Elmi.

Dunia's voice recites through my speakers, The mothers are the wisdom keepers, the cultural carriers, the teachers, our librarians. They hold people accountable. Many are mothers who have lost children to gun violence. They have children who are currently incarcerated. Many of them are fleeing domestic violence. They have been tortured in refugee camps, seen and survived the worst trauma. They teach one another, support one another, are there for one another.

The mothers prevent children from being apprehended. They teach young people about parenting. The teach boys in the remand about their culture. They say, this is who you are. This is who you are.

These mothers, many of them on assistance themselves, put together Elmi's bail plan. They gathered the money for him. They are women who live every day and face anti-Black racism. They are women who live every day and face Islamophobia. Some of them are barely paying their rent and yet they'll take their last dime to save a young African man.

They say, We feel responsible to Elmi. It is our responsibility as mothers, who are the natural leaders of our community, to ensure that every single Black African child is protected. He's our son, and we would expect people to help our son the same way we helped him.

It is the women who are behind Elmi.

Dunia says, As a young woman I'm learning a lot from the coalition in terms of motherhood, in terms of our culture, in terms of healing from trauma and creating a common memory.

Abdoul asked me last year when we were fighting for him, Will you remember me? I am haunted by his description of the cell, the names of the deported, the open grave. The Somali mothers give memory back to us. They will hold us all.

Fatuma brings her children to our emergency press conference in Halifax for Elmi. In Toronto, Elmi's mother speaks, surrounded by Somali mothers who dropped everything to come out, to wipe her tears and hold her hands.

Fatuma's son Zayden grabs a sign. It reads, Hey! Stop deporting child refugees! The newspaper runs a picture of Fatuma and her children with the headline "Nothing has changed."

And it's true, the system hasn't changed at all, not for all our ink and sweat and tears spilled. But we, we have changed. He is our son, say the Somali mothers and their love holds us all, heals us all, shows us the possibility for transformation. Again and again, I smile, thinking of them bursting into offices, yelling of freedom, and whisking away.

Time. Time is rushing ahead. On Friday, with only the weekend before Elmi is going to be deported, Dunia messages us around 2:00 p.m. The United Nations is requesting that Canada stop Elmi's deportation while they review the human rights issues in his case. On Thursday, Elmi's lawyer Idowu Ohioze argued for an emergency stay in court, but it's a long shot, almost impossible. There's no new arguments that can be made now.

We scramble into action. We need the media to know about the UN so if the court turns Elmi down, we can push throughout the weekend. Syed writes a press release in about ten minutes. We all jump in to edit. And then an hour later, disappointment. We were expecting it, but it's still crushing when the court decision comes back negative. The judge will not save Elmi. Now it all depends on the UN. We still have the weekend, I say, trying to be positive. We can run a campaign, tell Canada to listen to the UN. We are still thinking, planning, strategizing. We will not give up until the last minute.

And then, at 4:00 p.m., it feels like a miracle. Canada says they will accept the UN's request. We have swung between so many emotions in the last few hours, we are almost numb. But we did it, we did it, we did it.

We did it, for now.

Elmi is not safe as I write this. In the months after, there will be a struggle to get him bail. Desmond flies to Edmonton and gives up his rent money to add to what Dunia and Emmanuel have scraped together. Elmi does not have status. He cannot work or go to school. He does not have medical coverage. It is a condition of his bail that he attend rehab, but without coverage, how is he supposed to pay? Hands are washed of him over and over by the government.

Photos of Trudeau wearing blackface emerge in October. We are told we must forgive him because he has done so much for Black people. The names of Fatuma, of Abdoul, of Elmi, of the many others not yet known stretch before me. When Ralph Goodale is voted out on election night, I watch the reporters nearly crying on the news, paying tribute to what a great statesman he was, wondering whether he should be made a senator right away, mourning his loss.

What tears did he ever have for Elmi?

In Praise of First Girls

This article was first published in the Halifax Examiner *on April 28, 2019.*

Cassie joined our French class in Grade 9. She sat in front of me. I was drawn to her because of how proudly rude she was to the teacher. The teacher asked her, What is that in French? and she shot back, Shouldn't you know? You're the teacher.

I was a child from a strict immigrant home. My mother considered "jeez" a curse word. She considered a mark in the eighties a disappointment. She considered free time dangerous space that might be used to get pregnant. She consequently surveilled our comings and goings from the house. Anything after 9:00 p.m. was the time a "slattern" would come home. Anything after 8:00 a.m. was the time a slattern would lie in bed. My friends called her The General.

By May of the school year, she started complaining if we left our rooms because exams were close. Acceptable friends were those also in the advanced classes, whose parents she knew, who played in orchestras or band, or the children of congregation members at church.

Cassie was not an acceptable friend. She smoked on the front steps of the school. She told me that in the summer she would "hitchhike to Van." I had no idea what that meant. In gym class, she refused to wear gym clothes, pretended to have her period for weeks on end, and sat on the bleachers chewing gum. Paired up in French class, she would use the dialogues we were supposed to write to practice vocabulary words to construct subversive statements.

I was smitten.

Cassie was cool and dangerous. Given that I existed in fear of any call from the school to my mother and had an acute awareness of the shame I could bring upon her and that my mother was vocal about, I lived vicariously through Cassie's rebellions. I didn't have words like "subverting gender norms" or "transgressing social roles," but she was the first girl I was friends with where I recognized that these things existed and that she was crossing them. It was exciting and intoxicating.

Then there was the day when my mother gave her a ride, and the whole time Cassie sat in the backseat and talked about giving blowjobs. My mother was horrified. There was no context for this in my mother's world, a world where exams were a life-and-death matter that were the difference between Third World poverty and scholarships into white universities, and where respectability was ruthlessly policed because survival depended on being the right kind of women and the right kind of family.

There was no language in my mother's world — where tight lips and straight spines and dignity were the weapons against men who ran around, or left their families, or brought their women to the door — to name what it is that might make a young girl sit in a car with her friend's mother and talk about what she did with the older boys.

How could my mother respond when the only thing she was ever taught was to look the other way? How could she respond when what she knew about women protecting themselves was to shut daughters in rooms to study? She didn't even let us go to the mall. She was already appalled by Canadian friends who let their children have boyfriends or wear ripped jeans. How could she respond when, on the occasion of her leaving home, her mother came to her room, gave her a Bible and the Methodist Hymn Book, and told her if she read them every day, she would be safe?

I didn't have language either. One day, Cassie told me she was in the weight room with the football team. She was playing around with the weights and one of the older boys, in front of everyone, said, You would like a sport you can play on your back. Everyone laughed at her.

She laughed when she told me this, so I laughed too. It was a story she'd repeat to me more than once, searching for something from me that I couldn't see and didn't know how to give. Boys never even talked to me, the only girl who wasn't white. I was envious that they talked to her, that they grabbed at her, that they seemed to think she was attractive.

I couldn't see she was telling me because it hurt. I didn't know what those older boys were doing to her. I didn't know to say things to her like, he shouldn't have said that, or you deserve better than being treated like that, or even, that's not funny.

I know now that Cassie was raped in high school. I know now that in the backseat of my mother's car she was asking for help the only way she knew how. I know now that the things I was attracted to in her, the things that to me opened up exciting worlds, were expressions of trauma. I now know how she needed to be heard, but no one knew how to listen.

I think about them, those First Girls. The First Girls for sheltered girls who broke us out of our homes. I think about how those girls were sacrifices — not just to boys, or to schools that disciplined and suspended them, or to disapproving parents, but also to us, their friends who took from them the danger and had nothing to give back for the pain.

I think about how those girls, for us sheltered girls, are the story of the First Girl we knew who drank, or smoked, or talked back to teachers, and how for us they were so freeing. I think about how they were labelled. The ones called sluts, throwaways, troublemakers, bad girls, failures, behaviour problems, poor influences, trash. The ones whose suffering we couldn't see. The ones who are the bridges we crossed over on.

I'm in Vancouver at a youth poetry slam. I listen to high school girls do poems about rape culture, and slut shaming, and internalized misogyny, and racial identity, and growing up as immigrants, and I'm so goddamned glad they have the language that no one ever taught us. I'm so glad they know how to name and recognize things like sexual assault. I'm so glad they have other girls around them to tell them they're not at fault, and no boy has the right to shame you in the weight room. I'm so glad they have places to speak that aren't the backseat of the car.

I know just speaking and naming doesn't solve, or end, or even heal, but I'm so glad they at least have the words to start.

I wish I had the words when Cassie came to me. I wish someone had taught me, so I could have given her what she needed. I wish I could have been a first for her, the first friend who told her it was okay, the first friend to stand up for her. I wish I was the woman I am now, who would storm into that weight room, who would confront those boys in the hallways.

And maybe she, my first dangerous friend, maybe she is one of the reasons that I now can be the person who names, and shouts, and refuses, and talks back, and challenges, and uses my words freely.

Bless them, the First Girls who made us who we are. The girls who parents and teachers hated, the girls boys used and then made fun of, the girls who fought to assert themselves, and kept kicking, and kept their chins up. The girls who taught us to stand up for ourselves. The girls who aren't some moment in our stories who can then be discarded, but who were and are so valuable. Who gave us everything.

You are the doors we walked through.

FOR THE WOMEN
This poem was written from workshops with the women in Nova Institution.

First he took her body and he didn't ask to touch
And now they take her body and they lock it into cuffs
They say they have her on the camera with goods worth fifty
    bucks
There's laws to follow in this country, it's no excuse if life is rough

They say they caught her on parole with trace amounts of drugs
They say that looking at her record, the case is open-and-shut
She never had the words to even say what he had done
But now she's the one with sentences being given by a judge

And half the time nobody ever told her he was wrong
She's always been betrayed by every man she trusts

He says jail's easier for women so just say that it's her bust
He says he loves her so she takes the charges for her man
Her lawyer told her deal and she didn't understand
And they drag up all her past when they get her on the stand
They say she's unreliable, just check the tattoos on her hand

The crown says they won't charge her if she just tells on the gang
Now it's going round the neighbourhood they heard she's a rat
But police just turn their back 'cause she's Indigenous or Black
These men take what they want and then they throw her out like
    trash
And they all say she's worthless if she can't be flipped for cash

The workers take her baby 'cause they say that she can't bond
We know that wouldn't happen if she was middle-class and blond
But somehow they never showed when she was calling 911
And the day that she goes missing, nobody will respond

The headline says she was an addict and she was well known to
    the cops
And the picture that they use on the news is her latest mugshot

She's doing time on charges that never were her own
Her abusive boyfriend uses her apartment to hide the gun
She was the driver for the robbery we all know that he done
And now she writes him letters from her cell they go unanswered,
   every one

It's not like poor Black women smuggle drugs for fun
For men who send ten women through the airport and then go on
   the run
Men threatened and assaulted her 'til she swallowed the
   condoms
Now she's locked in federal prison while traffickers import tons
She just wants to feed her children, now cops tell her they'll be
   gone

Men exploit her body from the time that she is born
Her mother turns the other way to keep him safe and warm
He'll only do a year or two if he ever gets caught
While they've locked her down in seg when they accused her of
   assault
She's having flashbacks when they strip search her like rubbing
   wounds with salt
And now her body's being exploited one more time up in the
   courts

They tell her pay the victim surcharge, but she can't because
   she's poor
So she makes her money on the streets on the corner where she's
   forced
The cop took a so-called freebie but of course she can't report

She's never had a place to sleep that isn't someone else's floor
And then the undercover breaches her when she goes to make a
   score
They say that they'll convict her of committing welfare fraud
And now they're piling up the charges on her criminal record

They make her do the time then they start proceedings to deport

She lived her whole life here in foster care but nobody ever
    thought
To get her citizenship so they never sent the forms

They've chained her to the bed in the hospital ward
They punish her for having children, why can't she just abort
She'll only raise another generation for the taxpayer to support

And she's not the ideal victim so I guess it's all her fault

She's the 90 percent of victims doing time behind our walls
But when they talk about justice for rape survivors
They don't mean her at all

WE STILL RISE

We are the seat at the table
We descend from Sojourner Truth and Anne of Green Gables
We are Idle No More and Angela Davis
We are the grandmothers and the differently abled

We are the hair that refuses to be tamed
We are honouring Treaties and land claims
We are the movements that history never names

We are the waitresses and maids, the ponytails and braids
The queer women in Black Lives Matter holding up your parade
We are the femmes who refuse to be shamed

We are the Mohawk women calling the warriors to the barricades
We are Lemonade

We are equal work for equal pay
From homemakers to women stitching clothes for a dollar a day

We are Harriet Tubman toting that shotgun
When the men got too afraid

We are the heartbeat of the nation
We are most of the nurses and the educators
We are the women in prison raising their babies
We have been advised to be patient and we're tired of waiting
We are the anarchists and the peacemakers

We have been trained for resistance
We gain strength from walking with our sisters
We go to work and keep the house in visitor conditions
Unlike Charlie Sheen, we are actually winning

We are the anti-nuclear movement and abolition
We are the bosses called bitches for our ambition
We are plumbers, welders, and electricians
We run the whole office and are called assistants

We can make a can of soup stretch to feed a whole family for
    dinner
We are the grandmothers canning food for the winter
We are women's work like quilting and knitting
So you better believe we will make it through
With wisdom like Athena

We are the mothers of the Plaza de Mayo in Argentina
Latinas, Desis, and Filipinas

We are the love between Gabrielle and Xena
With power in our arms like Serena
We wear whatever the hell we want from hijabs to bikinis
We are the nannies and the cleaners, the peasants and the
    Zapatistas

We have survived the patrols at the border
The back-room abortions, the guards, and the wardens
We march against war for the mothers and orphans
We are the Guatemalan women surviving torture

We are the Indigenous women fighting for clean water
The trans women resisting the bathroom laws
We are the Jane Does in the missing person reports

We lead the peace movements for a better world for our
    daughters
We are the authors who had to take the names of men
We are feminist movements from Mexico to Uganda to Phnom
    Penh
We are the hashtag, we #BelieveWomen

We are sex workers unionizing
We are the queens and trans women at Stonewall fighting
The women in Saudi Arabia driving
We are the girls resisting sexist advertising
We are more than photoshop or vanity sizing

We are the Indigenous women who pushed for an inquiry

We are Queen Nzinga protecting her country from the colonizer
We are the environmental activists who chain themselves to
    bulldozers
The civil rights activists facing the fire hoses
The tenancy boards challenging public housing eviction notices
The women prisoners in Kingston when the men cut off their
    clothes
We are hunger strikes in prison for women's votes
And the force-feeding tubes shoved down their throats
We are the teen girls challenging sexist dress codes

We are the ninety-two-year-old woman walking during the
    Montgomery bus boycotts
The hidden figures behind the astronauts
The sewing machine and the pans and pots
We are suffragettes and les sans-culottes

We are the mothers of Trayvon Martin, Mike Brown, and Eric
    Garner
We are karma
And we have millennia of survival as our armour

We are Tina Turner finally leaving Ike
And we burn bright
With the fires of Joan of Arc and the strength of thousands of
    martyrs
We have justice as our target

We are calls for an end to poverty and for affordable housing
Reproductive rights and every life counting
Respect for Mother Earth and her surroundings
Access to treatment and an end to prison crowding

We are a living wage and basic allowance
And we are waving signs and fists, not drowning
We are singing songs of peace and shouting

We are generations of resistance that cannot be put down
We extend beyond elections and whoever's in the White House

We have been to the top of the mountain
We have survived, from genocides to witch trials
And they could not burn us out or wipe us out
Or push us aside

We are femmes, butches, trans, lesbians, women, and women-
     identified
We are standing here with pride
And still we rise
Still we rise
Still
We
Rise

✒ 8 ✒

Still Not Freedom

> Picture this woman
> saying *no* to the constant
> *yes* of slavery
> — Sonia Sanchez 2018, "Haiku and Tanka for Harriet Tubman"

I am thinking about the words of Judge Shaun Nakatsuru. A thirty-one-year-old woman named Josephine Pelletier from the Muskowekwan First Nation, brought before the court. The crown, asking for more punishment. Always more punishment, on top of the three years, on top of the long-term offender supervision.

We talk a lot about refusal. The power of rejecting complicity, of making a no. A no that is not just negative, but generative. Judge Nakatsuru's decision rejects prison as a place of healing, of help, or of necessity. What good is punishment? The word "good" in this question threatens to slip into the word "use," shifting the meaning of "what good does that do," into "what's the point?" But I want to hold onto the word good: What goodness does punishment bring? In refusing punishment, Nakatsuru chooses goodness instead. The decision ends:

> It is the most natural of human instincts to want to go home. Even when memories of home are at times tinged with sadness, fear, or regret. Because I am not talking about someone's actual home. Or a home from one's childhood. We all nurture in our heart the idea of "Home." The idea of home is about a place of safety. A refuge. A sanctuary. Where love resides. Home is a place of hope. A place of potential. A place where every one of us can feel like we can become better. Every one of us has such a home, Ms. Pelletier. Even if you live in a small room dimly lit by a bare light bulb hanging from the ceiling. Even if that home can only be conjured up in your imagination if you have the misfortune of

187

having to sleep in a dormitory or a shelter. Or on a steel cot in a prison cell.

After careful reflection, Ms. Pelletier, I am sending you home. I wish you all the best in your life. (*R. v. Pelletier*, Section 29, 30)

It is a hard task to live in prison, not just to wait for life to begin again after prison. A., behind glass in the provincial jail, tells me how scared he was when he found himself thinking, I hope I stay here for Christmas instead of federal prison, suddenly realizing he no longer imagined going home. I'm becoming institutionalized, he worries. Sometimes making a place your home — calling a prison cell your room — sometimes that is the most unsafe thing of all. Worse, because it is a necessity for survival.

∽ ∾

You deserve a cat, Sara texts me. I love her kittens so much, and she wants to get me a cat to love and be loved by.

Sara has been out about a year and a half. I met her in Nova Institution, where I got into trouble for hugging her after writing group. Or perhaps it was because I asked her about her life. Or perhaps because I told her to contact me when she got out. All these things, all these acts of kindness and humanity, are not permitted.

Sara gifts me my cat only months after she files a lawsuit against the guard who raped multiple women in the prison. The prison couldn't keep her safe. The prison doesn't even try to keep women safe. She had to investigate her own rapist, gather the evidence, subject herself to his harassing calls so they would be able to catch him. Such a brazen act of violence, out in the open, just another shift at work. Who would speak up? Who would listen?

It is out of this horror that Sara is bringing me life. She is not just gifting me a pet; she is remaking care. In a place where duty of care becomes assault, where touch is violation, where trust is exploitation, Sara still believes love can be given in tangible ways.

On the day the cat is ready to be taken home, Sara comes with me to collect her. Driving home with the terrified cat struggling in my arms, I am conscious of this small, shaking, fragile life. This is what it feels like to have another being's life quite literally in your hands. Even now, I feel the ghost of her fur, her warm body, the terrifying sense of the power I have over her. Ew, you're an animal kidnapper, says my partner, a die-hard hater of pet-dom. He's being facetious, but still, is this what it feels like to be a guard, to know that her food, her warmth, her being are directly under my control?

I think of the terror of homecoming for this cat, being taken from her mother and brought to a place with no familiar nurture, no comforting other fur, with all the wrong smells. How fervently, how helplessly, we believe home is safety — until it isn't. Until the punch, the nighttime trespass, the rejection. And after prison, how we believe homecoming is the end, how we forget prison still lingers in the running tap, the panic attack, the nightmare. How coming home is so often not what was promised, what was wished for. How often it sends people back.

That night, the cat hides behind shoes, won't come out for food. She remembers that awful drive. But the next morning she eats, and in a couple of days she stops wandering the rooms looking for her mother. If only all dislocation were so easily absorbed and forgotten.

I'm not there when Randy gets out. There's so much delay. First, after his appeal at the Supreme Court, the crown tries to remove his lawyer from the case. So that delays bail for a couple of months while they fight the removal. Then, when we make it to the bail hearing, the crown gives everyone a hard time, grilling us on the stand, calling his cousin's landlord to find out if she lives in public housing and if they're aware Randy is charged with murder — they claim she's violating the housing rules by offering for him to live with her. Randy feels like he'll be an imposition on his aunt, but it's obvious she wants him. Then there's the monitoring anklet, which has to be programmed from Colorado and transported from Toronto, and which costs $600 to install, and there's only one technician to install it, and that's three hours away from the jail. We hoped he'd be out for his birthday, but that comes and goes. We remake plans. Finally, a couple of weeks after the decision to release him on bail, the anklet arrives. It's late at night, and he can't leave without his sureties, so they drive to the jail two hours away to get him.

On the way home, they stop at a Burger King. Randy orders two bacon double cheeseburgers, without the bacon (he's Muslim.) Everybody laughs at this. Boy, you must have been in prison too long.

When Randy calls to tell me he's out, at first I don't recognize his voice. I've become so used to how it sounds filtered through the prison phone. Voices sound crisper, clearer in freedom.

But of course, this is still not freedom.

I get to Randy's aunt's house in the historical Black community of Cherry Brook right when they're leaving to go visit his mother's grave. We drive toward the church, but Randy's family lives all along the road on the way. We have to keep stopping, going into homes, greeting elderly aunts and cousins. It's a slow procession, like the stations of the cross or a pilgrimage, each stop another blessing. Reconnecting with the land, with the generations of his ancestors upon it, reconstituting life, reforming and remaking. Such an appropriate prelude to visiting the dead, to first honour the living. A reminder that we are still here, and we persist.

Then the graveyard, anchor of history in the community. His mother's grave, never visited until now. A marker — not of death, but of generations in this place, from this place. Another blessing for people dislocated and dispersed: to be close to one's dead. I will never be buried beside my ancestors here in this far-flung country. Oh, where my mother's bones go, I will follow. To walk upon this earth in this community, and to draw near to the past, a ritual of completion.

And after the graveyard there is the kitchen, with family coming in and out. Men bring clothes, disclaiming the act of shopping for another man, but they went to the mall anyway. Since Randy has been gone, pants have gotten tighter. We laugh at his skepticism, then there is pleasure at his appearance, clean, fresh, new. Remade. The kitchen, place of life and nourishment, filling us, filling us with joy. And in the middle of the back-and-forth and the laughter and the jokes and the noise all overflowing, his cousin pauses.

We made it out, he says. And again, We made it out.

And I think, isn't that the Black condition summed up, and it feels poignant for a moment, but this is not the time for reflection, no, not now, not surrounded by living, breathing, touching, speaking life.

But of course, there is later, when Randy tells me how his ankle is rubbed raw by his anklet put on too tightly, and in the telling, connects the wounds on his ankle with the enslaved ankles rubbed raw by shackles. He asks, Is this 1821 or 2021? The blistering is made worse by the heat and the sun. Freedom for Randy is spending his days outdoors, cutting the brush on the property, carving out the land, building space for his daughters to camp and roast marshmallows.

But this, this still isn't freedom. Not with an anklet it isn't, and not with an October trial hanging over him, and not with eight years lost to prison, and not with the crown still making him a monster, and not with the racism we can never make it out from, no matter where we go, how far we run, whatever escapes we engineer for ourselves.

I think about the term "halfway house," how strange it is. The idea of being halfway free. Musn't we be completely free for freedom to be freedom? I ask myself, but then I think that a yard with a anklet is a kind of freedom compared to a cell. It reminds me of the old puzzle about how far a fox can run into the woods — the answer is halfway, because after that he's running out. As though making it out is assumed once you get halfway in, as if no one will ever put you back, as if while you live under punishment and surveillance you are not always one step away, one mistake, from being taken back. Perhaps they should be called one-step houses.

In Kingston, at the site of the former Prison for Women, the women who were incarcerated in the prison have been fighting to build a healing garden.

What good can come from punishment?

Out of this place, where women died, where women suffered, where women were stripped and degraded and isolated, the women who came out want only a space where life can grow and be nurtured, fragile, tended by their own hands. "Nothing will come of nothing," King Lear says, but those who have been incarcerated so consistently make something from nothing. Creative meals from the noodle packs. Makeup from the coloured pencils in program. Love and solidarity out of abuse and hatred. Friendship from oppression. Sisterhood from captivity. The Strong Woman Song, written or gifted within those walls. Any good that comes — *any* good — they have forged themselves, *despite*.

Queen's University could have made the site flower when they owned it, could have returned it to the women, but instead they sold the site to a developer. I imagine this, the conversations about preserving the historic door locks, how to gut the place but leave some prison chic, that touch of edgy authenticity. Other homecomings, for the condo owners. A party story to titillate guests: I heard where my bathroom is used to be solitary confinement.

Perhaps there is no starker way to illustrate the grotesqueries of capitalism than to turn a prison into an unaffordable housing complex without blinking an eye, just as the residential school transforms into a prison, just as the plantation underlies the financial system. White supremacy always defaults to amnesia, and amnesia paves the way for innocence. My high school, built on a destroyed Métis village, while we went to class unaware.

I think about watching Alain Resnais' (1955) *Night and Fog*, how only a few short years after the Holocaust, the bricks from the walls of the concentration camps were gone, taken by the local people to rebuild their own homes. This is not the giving of new life, but its strangling. Those who pretended they did not see and hear the trains were close enough all along to take the building materials when the killing was over. Resnais shows us grass, reminds us there would have been no grass there, people would have eaten it. Oscar Wilde (2018, V:549) writes, "Every prison that men build is built with bricks of shame." I am not saying it is the same thing, but I am saying there is a continuum between building your garden wall with the bricks from a concentration camp and building a condo complex on top of places women screamed and wept.

There is a difference between bringing a garden to life from that place of suffering and confinement and making more luxury access. There is a difference between the life that is reclaimed from death, and the life that feeds itself by ignoring death. There is a difference between memory and development, understood in the capitalist sense, not in the sense of human goodness.

Garden or not, it is the women's fight, the belief that something good can be made, even in spaces of death and destruction, that is the flowering, the blooming. It is Randy in his yard until sunset and beyond, shaping the land on which escaped slaves rooted. It is Sara bringing care and cats, *it is time for you to have something to love*. Something near, something tangible, that cannot be separated from the voices on the phone, and the long drives through rural towns to the prison, and the tears in the courtroom.

Living with the aftermath of rape is not freedom. Living while prisons still stand is not freedom. Halfway is not freedom; neither is surveillance, looming trials, or renovating old prisons when everyone has been sent to new prisons elsewhere.

But cats and kitchens and gardens, perhaps they can be like the North Star, showing us how to get to freedom if we love each other, and fight, and remember.

What Is Desire to the Abolitionist?

Now, I like nice things too
  When I see Versace, I say, "ooooh!"
  — Lady Katalyst

My name, my full name, means "greatly desired." I assume this means a longed-for baby, and not a sexually attractive woman, but here we have already encountered a problem. For a girl and then a woman, to be an object of desire is complicated. And to be a Black woman, facing desire is even worse. In the white supremacist, capitalist, patriarchal imagination, desire for the Other is also twinned with disgust. We are the dirty secret of the colonizer, the hidden shame in the slave quarters, the youthful indiscretion of the racist politician.

But even as a baby, desire is complicated, bound up in parents' dreams for their child. And this, too, becomes fraught by colonial histories. My mother's only brother was born in a pre-independence Trinidad with no social resources. When it became apparent he was born with intellectual disabilities, my grandmother was advised to leave him at the hospital to die. She refused and fought, as a Black woman living in poverty, for him to be admitted to trade school. My family treated him as a blessing, but still, my mother recounted her fears that this was inheritable and her deep anxieties for each of our births. So, her desire for me never could be easy or simple, tinged with the fear of the wrong kind of baby. Desired, but not entirely — or, not in all possible entireties.

There has, of course, been much theorizing of desire. In religion, we are taught about the dangers of temptation, the treachery of our earthly bodies that insist on choosing sex, food, sleep over the rigours of the soul. Is heaven the place beyond desire, or the place where finally all our desires — finite on Earth — can be infinitely realized? Neuroscientists study what it is in our brains that makes us want and leaves us unsatisfied. Philosophers have debated how and why we want, whether it is natural or rational, the culture-boundness of our desires. Sociologists critique consumer culture under capitalism that induces desire in us, bringing us to want things fervently that we did not want until it was advertised to us, until we became aware of our inadequacies that only consumption can fix.

And of course, I want things too. Not so much material things, although I won't pretend I would turn them down, but what I could call social things. Recognition. I want the clicks on stories, and the positive reviews, and the awards, and the positions that come from these things. Of course I do. And wanting those things has always butted up against the thing in me that also desires freedom: my inability to keep my thoughts to myself and my mouth shut, my need to do things my own way, my scorn for those who do not "do the work" but succeed anyway. I consistently choose to do the things that make it impossible for me to have other things. But just because we have no option but to accept the consequences of our actions does not mean we like to do it.

I worry about these desires. I am torn by them. By this I mean I am aware in the deepest places of myself that the value of the work I do on state violence is surely not validated by how the rest of the world responds to it, but by how those who have turned to me for help or solidarity feel about it. This is not abstract theorizing: I know it because I have felt the deepest fulfilling joys of fighting these battles — the deportation, the wrongful conviction, the violation of rights — and being at least temporarily successful. In those moments, I have felt this is right, and good, and completing.

But yet, I remain a restless, unsatisfied person. These may be deep knowings, but it does not always mean they are functional ones. I can both know that it is more important to have the respect and comradeship of people in prison than to have an agent accept my book on prisons. But when that book was rejected, I closed my office door and cried, wondering what is wrong with me that I can never have anything. This is emotional hyperbole, because I have many things, much of which I want, but we are like this when we face disappointment. And I have cried on my floor when the jobs didn't come through, and I have found it hard to find pleasure in the compliments of those who matter to me in the face of rejection by those who do not.

I am aware that these wantings are not abolitionist. No, let me rephrase that. Perhaps they are abolitionist in that they are human, and part of abolition, I think, is recognizing that we are all broken and flawed, we all have the capacity for harm and have done it to others, and it is in awareness of our own faults that we locate compassion for others. So, to say I long for things I know I cannot and should not have, is to, for example, come into the same context as Oscar Wilde when he expresses, "each man kills the thing he loves" (2018, I: 37) in *The Ballad of Reading*

Gaol (as a child reading this poem, the central murder of a woman by her lover did not seem as disturbing to me as that line does now).

But they are not abolitionist in that they are desires brought forth in, or by, capitalism, with its hierarchies and classes and respectabilities telling me that to be without these things — degrees, titles, social position, etc. — is to lack worth. And so, I struggle with my wanting, with the gap between the things I know I believe and the parts of me that want all the things that make those beliefs impossible. Not that it is impossible to be an abolitionist and have a nice house, or a pleasurable job, or a vacation. But those things — or rather, the structures that surround them in our current social organization — inescapably come into conflict, in the getting of them, with the commitments required to bring a different world into being.

It sounds like I am suggesting the abolitionist world is a dour one of deprivation; a trap more than one revolutionary movement has fallen into in rooting out bourgeois pleasure and ending in mass executions and re-educations. No, it is not that we want to persecute desire. It is that we want those things not to have to be desired because they are a given. A safe home for everyone. The opportunity to work in autonomous ways for everybody. Free education for all who want it. I am talking more here about the internal struggle, the sense of failing one's own values, the impossibility at so many times of fitting what you know to be right beside the sacrifices you must take to get it, and the resentment of that.

Abolition is a reorientation to the world. As Ruth Wilson Gilmore (2022) writes, "Abolition requires that we change one thing: everything" (back cover copy). We understand this applies to all our institutions — not just prisons but the culture that brings prisons into being. To end the prison, we must end punishment and our vindictive desire for punishment. To end punishment, we must think about who we punish and why. To do that, we must think about housing and who doesn't have it and who is hassled by the police when they do not have it. We must think about land and our relation to it, and why settler colonialism sees land as something to extract from. We must think about power and control. And we must also think about ourselves, how we benefit from these systems and how we want those benefits for ourselves.

To think about this is to get perilously close to purity discourse, to the endless flogging of ourselves, to reification of guilt and anxiety. And that is not what I am trying to build here at all, a world where we brutally examine ourselves for any sign of promiscuous, undisciplined desire. It is too close to punishment itself. It is not the desire I am troubled by, but the causing of it. Why is it that a university job eluding me can shatter my self-worth and sense of being in the world at the same time as I know these institutions are not built to care about the people and issues and world that I care about? Why is stopping the deportation or winning the appeal not enough? I do not mean "enough" in the sense of it being finished justice, for having watched Derek Chauvin be convicted we know justice is never brought by one moment, one verdict, one policy change. I mean "enough" in my own internal sense of fulfillment.

I think what I am really asking is, what does it mean to live in the world as an abolitionist when we know we will not see the world we labour to build in our own lifetimes? Abolition in our current time is inherently believing in something we will always fall short from. We believe prisons must fall, but in the meantime, there is money to be put on the phones and canteen, which paradoxically feeds the prison industrial complex. But that small pleasure of canteen is what makes life inside a little more bearable. We would not ask that to be given up on the theoretical ideal of resistance.

We must learn to make a home in this falling short. We must learn to make a home, in our homes, the foundations of the world we envision. As Mariame Kaba (2021) reminds us, over and over, we practise abolition every day in practical ways by challenging ourselves to think differently about conflict, to not see accountability as chastisement but as transformative, to move beyond shame in our failed or incomplete attempts at reparation. We practise abolition by organizing: bringing the groceries, and speaking with our relatives about sexual violence when they have never voiced their trauma, and banding together in our building to reject the landlord. We practise it lying under the deportation van, and in the protest outside the prison, and in the rides we share to these places as we build collectivity and mutual aid. In a selfish society, it takes practice to unlearn our wants, to find new things to reach toward. It is not stripping away what we want but filling ourselves with something different, with love for each other and shared successes.

I know my wanting has a history. I think there is maybe always guilt to wanting as a Black person, as we are always aware that everything we have, even breath, was won for us by the suffering of our ancestors. However bad we have it, we are taught, it is nothing on what those of generations before endured. Paradoxically, it is because of this suffering that we are also taught success is a responsibility; we owe it to them to achieve the things they could not. *I am the hope and the dream of the slave.* But we cannot imagine our dreaming without slavery. We cannot think of our freedom without remembering our unfreedom. There are some of us who respond to this history by embracing the getting. Get your bag, girl! Our mansion is a slap in the face to the spectre of the slave master. I think of that Dave Chappelle sketch about the time haters, travelling through time to shoot slave masters, We travelled all the way back through time to call you a cracker. Chappelle captured that fundamental desire, the vindication and joy of revenge. It is not abolitionist, but it is satisfying, and this, too, is abolitionist struggle as we know that abolition is also for the police who murder Black people. Even as we feel that as long as there are prisons, surely those are the people who should be in them.

But Black capitalism is not a substitute for white capitalism — or rather, it is only substitution. Now the ANC and not a white person can preside over miners being gunned down at Marikana. And Black people can profit from it too. This is not freedom. And so, to desire freedom we must eventually desire something else, something beyond. And even in abolitionist circles this is a tension between what we say we believe in and the difficulties of living up to it when there are always others who will take those opportunities, and receive that praise, and live easier for it.

Without that beyond, my desires make me restless, unhappy. Perhaps ironically, I suspect part of my drive to activism is rooted in this sense of discontent. The solution is not asceticism; I believe it is richness. But a richness located in each other, not in self.

We think of ending desire as a punishment, perhaps, as self-discipline and deprivation. But what would desire look like in a world without punishment? If we learned to be generous with ourselves. If we did not believe indulgence must be met with reduction. If we did not feel we failed ourselves when we fall short and then bitterly reproach ourselves. Would our desires then morph into something gentler?

Perhaps abolition is also the uncovering of our autonomous desires, which have been muffled by capitalism, racism, patriarchy, etc. Perhaps it is as simple as returning to the most basic of needs: food, shelter, companionship. Perhaps in reshaping our wanting, we reshape the world. There is a place for desire in an abolitionist world, at least when desire is pleasure and love and freedom.

TO ALL MY PEOPLE DOING TIME

T. comes into prison a proud white supremacist
He's got swastikas tattooed on his neck and KKK on the knuckles
    on his fist
And the last prison he was in, there's a guy he already killed
But there's a Black guy on the range and somehow they start to
    chill
He says just cover that shit up around me if we're going to
    coexist
And they're both doing life over blood that they have spilled
And slowly, slowly, somehow their friendship starts to build

Well T. gets transferred out and from the depths he sends a letter
Thank you for your friendship, for helping me be better
He says, my sister was gang-raped at a party by Black guys
And I decided every single Black guy was the same in my eyes
I was so angry that my hate was twisting me inside
Thank you for showing me another way
Thank you for saving me

If we've never struggled to make a change
What do we know of bravery?
What do we know about transformation
In these places where we're breaking people down

D. is waiting in the hole, it's been seven or eight months now
One day he loses it in his cell and starts trashing everything
    around
And then he hears a knock
And he thinks what now
I can't take anymore, this pressure has to stop
And a hand reaches through his slot

And D.'s on edge, thinking it's someone here to take a shot
The guy's high up in a gang, a soldier at the top
But he opens up his fist and there's a jade and black crucifix
And all he says is simply, I thought you needed this

What do we know of human kindness and the places it exists
When we sentence people to life and say their humanity's
eclipsed
And we send them behind the walls and condemn them to the
abyss

And Massacre toasts bread and hides it in the fridge
He grew up on a remote reserve with no food when he was a kid
Cap'n Crunch at Christmas was what his mother knew of gifts
Uncles struggling with their own addictions who taught him how
to fix
When residential schools left generations broke in bits
And the other guys bug him now because he only owns one lime-
green pair of sweats
So when someone offers him twenty dollars, that's as good as it
gets
They ask him to heat up butter in the microwave and throw it in a
face
And he gets dragged off to solitary, but for him it's not a waste
Because twenty dollars is enough to get a couple weeks canteen

What do we know of desperation when our stomach's full when
we go to sleep?
What do we know of wounding where the trauma runs so deep?

And so we lock people down, never allowed out in the open
But the light gets through the cracks in the places that we're
broken
So many lives that disappear and their stories are unspoken
So we never hear of resilience, of creativity, of hoping

I'm reading Facebook and I see a status that touches me
profoundly
I love my murderer friends, one of the women proclaims proudly
And everyone reacts with horror and disgust
But she says I spent years in with these women, the only ones I
could trust
And I'm not going to throw them under the bus, I'm not going to
abandon

You don't know what's inside people when you just judge them at
  random
And I know what she means 'cause murderer is the worst label
When we couple it with love, it makes our judgements unstable
So we condemn a woman loving deeper than we're able
As if murderer and loved one can never be connected

What do we know of affection when we don't live together in
  oppression?
Everything I know about forgiveness, it was prisoners taught the
  lesson

And I keep suggesting to a teenage prisoner he go outside for
  exercise
You'll get sick, I tell him, you'll disappear inside depression
And finally he tells me that a year after he'd been inside
He was let out in the yard and bent and touched a blade of grass
And then he overheard a conversation between guards
That kid's been in so long, he's happy just to touch the ground
And after that it was too hard, so he just stays on his range now
What do we know of freedom when we've never been held down?

And there's a young Mi'kmaw man who calls me and tells me that
  he's fine
And then I link him to his mother and he starts crying on the line
And he tells her he almost died because he drank hand sanitizer
What do we know of pain when numb's the only option for
  survival?

And there are teenagers inside who are shaking on arrival
And I think it's obscene that every courtroom has a Bible
And then we sentence human beings to places where if they're
  suicidal
They strip them of their clothes and throw them into solitary
  confinement
And once you get a record, it's a judgement that is final
There's no supports when you get out, so you're forced to repeat
  the cycle
What do we know of forgiveness when our vengeance still is
  primal?

And there's so many minds going to waste full of knowledge that
    is vital
Who knows if the cure for AIDS is in a mind that's sitting idle?
And in spite of their situation, they're still maintaining their
    humanity

I host a radio show with prisoners and some people complain
    about profanity
And I tell them music is the only thing that helps them keep their
    sanity
Actually, I say, we have people calling in from solitary
    confinement
So excuse them if they don't quite meet your standards of
    refinement
And they're assigned to jobs in sweatshops making products on
    consignment
Or they're deprived of medication and you want them to be
    silenced?
What do you know of self-expression when you've never had to
    fight to write?

And there are suicidal women forced to sleep without their
    mattresses
Dehumanizing conditions seen as just everyday practices
People talk of justice as if it's just a scale that balances
While families and communities are grieving all the absences
If we've never sat inside a cell, then what do we possibly know of
    damages?

But I've seen things come out of prison that I would call
    miraculous
Love, forgiveness, resilience, generosity, and thankfulness
What I know of being human comes from being a prison activist
To all my people doing time, thank you for making me
    compassionate

GOODNIGHT JAIL
Based on Goodnight Moon *(1947) by Margaret Wise Brown*

In a provincial jail there's a little room
With a toilet and a sink and a smell of mildew

And a slit of a window with a sliver of the moon
And a radio on a shelf playing a tune

And a metal cot, and a metal slot
And a night that's either too cold or too hot

And an officer in the spot by the stairs
And three more guards sitting in chairs

And the shadow of the laws that put people in there

And the eye of the camera watching you sitting
And a photocopied picture of your mother and children

And a heart with a hole for the loved ones you're missing
And restless dreams where you wake up shivering

And a door with a lock, and a window with bars
And a corner of the sky showing just one star

And a comb, and a brush, and a toilet that won't flush
And a guard on his rounds ordering hush

So good night room like a little tomb
Good night window barely showing the moon

Good night laws that aren't changing soon
Good night radio, good night news

Good night cot, good night slot
Good night down in solitary, where the world forgot

Good night sheets tied up in a knot
Good night bad dreams and regretful thoughts
Good night clanging doors and the camera shot

Good night locks, good night clocks
Good night countdown to the day you get out of the box

Good night mildew, good night mould
Good night lights on all night down in the hole

Good night heart with its little hole
Good night heat, good night cold

Good night foam mattress, good night comb
Good night to the crumpled picture of home

Good night dripping sink and toilet that won't flush
And good night to the officers ordering hush

Good night patrols, good night stare
Good night outside, goodnight air

Good night love, good night care
Good night prisoners everywhere

References

Abdi v. Canada (Public Safety and Emergency Preparedness), 2018. FC 733, Recorded Entries. May 29, 2018.

Abdillahi, Idil, and El Jones. 2020. "No Life Left Behind." Webcast. https://www.facebook.com/events/d41d8cd9/no-life-left-behind-conversations-about-lifers/321166949003957/

Abdillahi, Idil, and Rinaldo Walcott. 2019. *BlackLife: Post-BLM and the Struggle for Freedom.* Winnipeg: ARP Books.

"Abolition in So-Called Canada Syllabus." 2020. https://static1.squarespace.com/static/5e87d4e1eaa9be375415ac85/t/5f28235f7b9431047e44d0fd/1596466020029/ABSC2020b.pdf

Adjei, Paul B. 2012. "When Blackness Shows Up Uninvited: Examining the Murder of Trayvon Martin through Fanonian Racial Interpellation." In *Contemporary Issues in the Sociology of Race and Ethnicity: A Critical Reader,* edited by George S. Dei and Meredith Lordan. New York: Peter Lang Publishing.

Alexander, Michelle. 2012. *The New Jim Crow: Mass Incarceration in the Age of Colorblindness,* revised edition. New York: New Press.

Arbour, Louise. 1996. *Commission of Inquiry into Certain Events at the Prison for Women in Kingston.* Ottawa: Canada Communication Group C Publishing. http://www.justicebehindthewalls.net/resources/arbour_report/arbour_rpt.htm

Bailey, Moya. 2021. *Misogynoir Transformed: Black Women's Digital Resistance.* New York: New York University Press.

Barker, Joanne. 2008. "Gender, Sovereignty, Rights: Native Women's Activism against Social Inequality and Violence in Canada." *American Quarterly* 60, 2.

Bousquet, Tim. 2018. "Habeas Corpus Hearing Illuminates Jail Condition." *Halifax Examiner,* September 18. https://www.halifaxexaminer.ca/province-house/habeas-corpus-hearing-illuminates-jail-conditions/

Brand, Dionne. 1990. *No Language Is Neutral.* Toronto: Coach House Press.

___. 2001. *A Map to the Door of No Return: Notes to Belonging.* Toronto: Doubleday Canada.

Brooks, Tanya. 2007. "Just Like Me." In *Words Without Walls: Writing and Art by Women in Prison in Nova Scotia,* 35. Books Beyond Bars.

Brown, Michelle. 2009. *The Culture of Punishment: Prison, Society, and Spectacle.* New York: New York University Press.

Browne, Simone. 2015. *Dark Matters: On the Surveillance of Blackness.* Durham: Duke University Press.

Butler, Judith. 1993. "Endangered/Endangering: Schematic Racism and White Paranoia." In *Reading Rodney King/Reading Urban Uprising,* edited by Robert Gooding-Williams. New York: Routledge.

Cacchione, Felix. 2020. "Summary of Investigation SIRT File # 2020-001 Halifax Regional Police January 16, 2020." Submitted October 5, 2020. https://sirt.novascotia. ca/sites/default/files/reports/Summary%20of%20Investigation%202020-001.pdf

CAEFS (Canadian Association of Elizabeth Fry Societies). 2020. "Former Correctional Officer at the Nova Institution for Women Arrested on Charges of Sexual Assault Against Prisoners." Press release, May 7. https://ac935091-bf76-4969-8249-ae3a107fca23.filesusr.com/ugd/d2d30e_9f4e17a78edd446f9d0f59efaa60de3b.pdf?index=true

Carby, Hazel. 1997. "White Woman Listen! Black Feminism and the Boundaries of Sisterhood." In *Black British Feminism: A Reader,* edited by Heidi Safia Mirza. New York: Routledge.

CBC. 2015. "Quebec Judge Orders Review of Inmate's Grievance over Porn TV Channels in Prison." August 7. https://www.cbc.ca/news/canada/montreal/quebec-judge-orders-review-of-inmate-s-grievance-over-porn-tv-channels-in-prison-1.3183996

Clairmont, Donald H., and Dennis William MacGill. 1999. *Africville: The Life and Death of a Canadian Black Community.* Toronto: Canadian Scholars' Press.

Clarke, George Elliott. 2012. *Directions Home: Approaches to African-Canadian Literature.* Toronto: University of Toronto Press.

Collins, Patricia Hill. 2000. *Black Feminist Thought: Knowledge, Consciousness, and the Politics of Empowerment,* second edition. New York: Routledge.

Cossman, Brenda. 2002. "Family Feuds: Neo-Liberal and Neo-Conservative Visions of the Reprivatization Project." In *Privatization, Law, and the Challenge to Feminism,* edited by Brenda Cossman and Judy Fudge. Toronto: University of Toronto Press.

Coulthard, Glen. 2014. *Red Skin, White Masks: Rejecting the Colonial Politics of Recognition.* Minneapolis: University of Minnesota Press.

Crenshaw, Kimberlé Willams. 1989. "Demarginalizing the Intersection of Race and Sex: A Black Feminist Critique of Antidiscrimination Doctrine, Feminist Theory and Antiracist Policies," *University of Chicago Legal Forum* 1.

____. 1997. "Beyond Racism and Misogny: Black Feminism and 2 Live Crew." In *Feminist Social Thought: A Reader,* edited by Diana Tietjens Meyers. New York: Routledge.

CSC (Correctional Service of Canada). 1990. *Creating Choices: The Report of the Task Force on Federally Sentenced Women.* April. https://www.csc-scc.gc.ca/women/toce-eng.shtml

____. 2016. Commissioner's Directive 710-8: Private Family Visits. July 26, 2016. https://www.csc-scc.gc.ca/acts-and-regulations/710-8-cd-eng.shtml#d3

Culhane, Claire. 1979. *Barred from Prison: A Personal Account.* Vancouver: Pulp Press Limited.

____. 1984. *Still Barred from Prison: Social Injustice in Canada.* Montreal: Black Rose Books Ltd.

____. 1991. *No Longer Barred from Prison: Social Injustice in Canada.* Montreal: Black Rose Books Ltd.

Cunningham, Alison, and Linda Baker. 2004. "Invisible Victims: The Children of Women in Prison." Voices for Children. http://citeseerx.ist.psu.edu/viewdoc/download?doi=10.1.1.555.9642&rep=rep1&type=pdf

Davis, Angela. 1971. *If They Come in the Morning: Voices of Resistance.* New York: The Third Press.

____. 2011. *Are Prisons Obsolete?* New York: Seven Stories Press.

Devet, Robert. 2017. "Help End Exploitative Phone Charges in Nova Scotia Provincial Jails." *Nova Scotia Advocate,* April 2. https://nsadvocate.org/2017/04/02/op-ed-help-end-exploitative-phone-charges-in-nova-scotia-provincial-jails/

Donovan, Laura. 2016. "'Prison Bae' Ignores a Terrifying Reality for Women in Prison." *Attn* June 1. https://archive.attn.com/stories/8762/prison-bae-ignores-sexual-as-sault-problem-female-prisoners-face

Dryden, OmiSoore. 2020. "Racist Responses to COVID-19 Place Us All at Greater Risk." *Chronicle Herald,* September 2. https://www.thechronicleherald.ca/opinion/local-perspectives/omisoore-dryden-racist-responses-to-covid-19-place-us-all-at-greater-risk-492256/

Elizabeth Fry Societies of Mainland Nova Scotia and Wellness Within. 2017. "Trans Women Are Women." Press release, September 19. https://static1.squarespace.com/static/5a17715d8dd04195b6708c76/t/5a653dcfec212d8a1b96080f/1516584400495/press+release+re+Trans+women+are+women.pdf

Ellison, Ralph, and Richard Kostelanetz. 1989. "An Interview with Ralph Ellison." *The Iowa Review* 19.3. https://doi.org/10.17077/0021-065X.3779

Faith, Karlene. 2011. *Unruly Women: The Politics of Confinement and Resistance.* New York: Seven Stories Press.

Foucault, Michel. 1995. *Discipline and Punish: The Birth of the Prison,* translated by Alan Sheridan, second ed. New York: Vintage-Random House.

Fanon, Frantz. 1968. *Black Skin, White Masks.* London: MacGibbon & Kee.

Garfinkel, Harold. 1961. "Conditions of Successful Degradation Ceremonies." *American Journal of Sociology* 61, 5.

Gilmore, Ruth Wilson. 2022. *Change Everything: Racial Capitalism and the Case for Abolition.* Chicago: Haymarket Books.

Halifax Examiner. 2020. "Black Lives Matter in Prison Too." June 14. https://www.halifaxexaminer.ca/featured/black-lives-matter-in-prison-too/

Hanington, Deni. 2020. "From the Inside Out: Effects of Parental Incarceration on Children." *Canadian Journal of Family and Youth* 12, 2.

Harney, Stefano, and Fred Moten. 2013. *The Undercommons: Fugitive Planning & Black Study.* New York: Minor Compositions.

Hartman, Saidiya V. 1997. *Scenes of Subjection: Terror, Slavery, and Self-Making in Nineteenth-Century America.* Oxford: Oxford University Press.

___. 2007. *Lose Your Mother: A Journey Along the Atlantic Slave Trade Route.* New York: Farrar, Straus, and Giroux.

Hesse-Biber, Sharlene Nagy, and Patricia Leavy. 2008. "Historical Context of Emergent Methods and Innovation in the Practice of Research Methods." In *Handbook of Emergent Methods,* edited by Sharlene Nagy Hesse-Biber and Patricia Leavy. New York: Guildford Press.

hooks, bell. 1989. *Talking Back: Thinking Feminist, Thinking Black.* Boston: South End Press.

___. 2000. *Feminism Is for Everybody: Passionate Politics.* London: Pluto Press.

Housman, A.E. 1898. "On Moonlit Heath and Lonesome Bank," in A *Shropshire Lad.* London: Grant Richards. https://babel.hathitrust.org/cgi/pt?id=uiug.30112040195106&view=1up&seq=1

Hughes, Langston. 1994. *The Collected Poems of Langston Hughes.* New York: Alfred A. Knopf.

Hughes, Sam. D. 2020. "Release Within Confinement: An Alternative Proposal for Managing the Masturbation of Incarcerated Men in U.S. Prisons." *Journal of Positive Sexuality* 6, 1.

Hurston, Zora Neale. 2018. *Barracoon: The Story of the Last "Black Cargo."* New York:

HarperLuxe.

Iftene, Adeline. 2019. *Punished for Aging: Vulnerability, Rights, and Access to Justice in Canadian Penitentiaries.* Toronto: University of Toronto Press.

J.C. 2019. "Christmas in Prison." *Halifax Examiner,* December 24. https://www.halifax-examiner.ca/featured/christmas-in-prison/

Jackson, Michael. 2002. *Justice Behind the Walls: Human Rights in Canadian Prisons.* Madiera Park: Douglas and McIntyre. http://www.justicebehindthewalls.net/book.asp?cid=1

James, Joy. 2020. "Airbrushing Revolution for the Sake of Abolition." *Black Perspectives,* July 20. https://www.aaihs.org/airbrushing-revolution-for-the-sake-of-abolition

John, Arit. 2014. "A Recent History of Free #PrisonBae Campaigns and Backlashes." *The Atlantic,* June 20. https://www.theatlantic.com/culture/archive/2014/06/a-recent-history-of-free-prisonbae-campaigns-and-backlashes/373147/

Johnson, Val Marie. 2019. "'I'm Sorry Now We Were So Very Severe': 1930's Colonizing Care Relations between White Anglican Women Staff and Inuvialuit, Inuinnait, and Iñupiat People in an 'Eskimo Residential School.'" *Feminist Studies* 45, 2–3.

Jones, El. 2018. "The Prisoners at the Burnside Jail Are Engaged in a Non-Violent Protest; Here Is Their Statement." *Halifax Examiner,* August 19. https://www.halifaxexaminer.ca/province-house/the-prisoners-at-the-burnside-jail-are-engaged-in-a-non-violent-protest-here-is-their-statement/

Kaba, Mariame. 2021. *We Do This 'Til We Free Us: Abolitionist Organizing and Transforming Justice.* Chicago: Haymarket Books.

Kelley, Robin D.G. 1996. *Race Rebels: Culture, Politics, and the Black Working Class.* New York: Free Press.

Kitossa, Tamari. 2020. "Authoritarian Criminology and Racist Statecraft: Rationalizations for Racial Profiling, Carding and Legibilizing the Herd." *Decolonization of Criminology and Justice* 2, 1.

Lamble, Sarah. 2015. "Transforming Carceral Logistics: Ten Reasons to Dismantle the Prison Industrial Complex Using a Queer and Trans Analysis." In *Captive Genders: Trans Embodiment and the Prison Industrial Complex,* edited by Eric A. Stanley and Nat Smith. Chico: AK Press.

Lawrence, Bonita. 2003. "Gender, Race, and the Regulation of Native Identity in Canada and the United States: An Overview." *Hypatia* 18, 2.

Lawrence, D.H. 1960. *Lady Chatterley's Lover.* London: Penguin Books.

Lee, Butch. 2000. *Jailbreak Out of History: The Re-Biography of Harriet Tubman.* Montreal: Kerseblebdeb Publishing.

Lee, Eumi K. 2018. "Monetizing Shame: Mugshots, Privacy, and the Right to Access." *Rutgers Law Review* 70, 557.

Leroux, Darryl. 2019. *Distorted Descent: White Claims to Indigenous Identity.* Winnipeg: University of Manitoba Press.

lilley, pj. 2014. "Prisoners' Justice Day: A Retrospective Montage." *Radical Criminology: An Insurgent Journal* 4. http://journal.radicalcriminology.org/index.php/rc/article/view/68

Lorde, Audre. 1984. *Sister Outsider: Essays and Speeches.* Berkeley: The Crossing Press.

Lowe, Lisa. 1996. *Immigrant Acts: On Asian American Cultural Politics.* Durham: Duke University Press.

___. 2015. *The Intimacies of Four Continents.* Durham: Duke University Press.

MacEachern, Meghan. 2019. "Exploring Women-Centred, Holistic, and Trauma-Informed Programming for Provincially Incarcerated Women in Canada: A Case

Study of the New Brunswick Women's Correctional Centre." MA thesis, Saint Mary's University. http://library2.smu.ca/bitstream/handle/01/28735/MacEachern_Meghan_MASTERS_2019.pdf?isAllowed=y&sequence=1

Maynard, Robyn. 2017. *Policing Black Lives: State Violence in Canada from Slavery to the Present.* Halifax: Fernwood Publishing.

___. 2019. "Black Life and Death across the US-Canada Border: Border Violence, Black Fugitive Belonging, and a Turtle Island View of Black Liberation." *Critical Ethnic Studies* 5, 1–2.

Maynard, Robyn, and Leanne Betasamosake Simpson. 2020. "Towards Black and Indigenous Futures on Turtle Island: A Conversation." In *Until We Are Free: Reflections on Black Lives Matter in Canada,* edited by Rodney Diverlus, Sandy Hudson, and Syrus Marcus Ware. Regina: University of Regina Press.

McClelland, Alexander, and Alex Luscombe. 2020. "Policing the Pandemic: Tracking the Policing of COVID-19 Across Canada." *Borealis* V8. https://doi.org/10.5683/SP2/KNJLWS

McCurdy, Howard. 2001. "Africville: Environmental Racism." In *Faces of Environmental Racism: Confronting Issues of Global Justice,* edited by Laura Westra and Bill E. Lawson, second edition. Washington: Rowman and Littlefield.

McIvor, Sharon Donna. 2004. "Aboriginal Women Unmasked: Using Equality Litigation to Advance Women's Rights." *Canadian Journal of Women and the Law* 16, 1.

McKendy, John P. 2006. "'I'm Very Careful About That': Narrative and Agency of Men in Prison." *Discourse & Society* 17, 4.

McKittrick, Katherine. 2006. *Demonic Grounds: Black Women and the Cartographies of Struggle.* Minneapolis: University of Minnesota Press.

___. 2013. "Plantation Futures." *Small Axe* 17, 3.

Milburn, Chris. 2019. "'Criminal Element' Sent to ER Puts Docs in Dicey Spot." *Chronicle Herald,* November 14. https://www.thechronicleherald.ca/opinion/local-perspectives/dr-chris-milburn-criminal-element-sent-to-er-puts-docs-in-dicey-spot-376037/

Monture, Patricia A. 2006. "Confronting Power: Aboriginal Women and Justice Reform." *Canadian Women's Studies* 25, 3–4.

Morgan, Anthony. 2018. "'Being Big and Black Makes It Hard to Breathe in Canada Too': Why 'I Can't Breathe' Isn't a Foreign Phenomenon." CBC (*Out in the Open*), February 16. https://www.cbc.ca/radio/outintheopen/last-words-1.4512355/being-big-and-black-makes-it-hard-to-breathe-in-canada-too-why-i-can-t-breathe-isn-t-a-foreign-phenomenon-1.4512813

Moten, Fred. 2003. *In the Break the Aesthetics of the Black Radical Tradition.* Minneapolis: University of Minnesota Press.

Mugabo, Délice. 2019. "On Haunted Places: Encountering Slavery in Quebec." In *Black Writers Matter,* edited by Whitney French. Regina: University of Regina Press.

Mullings, Dolores, with Renee Mullings-Lewis. 2013. "How Black Mothers 'Successfully' Raise Children in the 'Hostile' Canadian Climate." *Journal of the Motherhood Initiative* 4, 2.

Mussell, Linda. 2020. "Disrupting Intergenerational Incarceration." Paper presented at: *Wellness Within 2020 Annual Conference: Breaking It Down, Building Something New, Online, November 25, 2020.* https://wellnesswithinns.org/annual-conference

National Post. 2014. "Paul Bernardo Intends to Marry 30-Year-Old Ontario Woman Who Thinks Notorious Sex Killer Is Innocent: Report." July 3. https://nationalpost.com/news/canada/paul-bernardo-intends-to-marry-30-year-old-ontario-woman-who-thinks-notorious-sex-killer-is-innocent-report

Office of the Correctional Investigator. 2012. "Spirit Matters: Aboriginal People and the Corrections and Conditional Release Act." *OCI.* https://www.oci-bec.gc.ca/cnt/rpt/pdf/oth-aut/oth-aut20121022-eng.pdf

___. 2013. "Risky Business: An Investigation of the Treatment and Management of Chronic Self-Injury Among Federally Sentenced Women." *OCI.* https://www.oci-bec.gc.ca/cnt/rpt/oth-aut/oth-aut20130930-eng.aspx

___. 2020. "Annual Report: Office of the Correctional Investigator." *OCI.* https://www.oci-bec.gc.ca/cnt/rpt/pdf/annrpt/annrpt20192020-eng.pdf

Palmater, Pamela. 2014. "Genocide, Indian Policy, and Legislated Elimination of Indians in Canada." *Aboriginal Policy Studies* 3, 3.

___. 2017. "Death by Poverty: The Lethal Impacts of Colonialism." In *Power and Resistance*, sixth edition, edited by Wayne Antony, Jessica Antony, and Les Samuelson. Winnipeg: Fernwood Publishing.

Parkes, Debra. 2014. "The Punishment Agenda in the Courts." *The Supreme Court Law Review: Osgoode's Annual Constitutional Cases Conference* 67.

___. 2018. "Mandatory Minimum Sentences for Murder Should Be Abolished." *Globe and Mail,* September 24. https://www.theglobeandmail.com/opinion/article-mandatory-minimum-sentences-for-murder-should-be-abolished/

___. 2019. "Punishment and Its Limits." 88 Sup Ct L Rev 351. 351-367. https://commons.allard.ubc.ca/cgi/viewcontent.cgi?article=1482&context=fac_pubs

Patterson, Orlando. 2018. *Slavery and Social Death: A Comparative Study, with a New Preface.* Cambridge: Harvard University Press.

Philip, Marlene NourbeSe. 2005. "Fugues, Fragments and Fissures—A Work in Progress." *Anthurium: A Caribbean Studies Journal:* 3, 2. https://anthurium.miami.edu/articles/abstract/10.33596/anth.51/

Piché, Justin, and Kevin Walby. 2010. "Problematizing Carceral Tours." *The British Journal of Criminology* 50, 3.

Pollack, Shoshana, and Tiina Eldridge. 2015. "Complicity and Redemption: Beyond the Insider/Outsider Research Dichotomy." *Social Justice* 42, 2.

R. v. Pelletier, 2016. ONCJ 628. October 12.

Rao, Santina. 2020. "I Am Worth RESPECT." *Halifax Examiner,* June 25. https://www.halifaxexaminer.ca/featured/santina-rao-i-am-worth-respect/

Razack, Sherene. 2002. "When Place Becomes Race." In *Race, Space and the Law: Unmapping a White Settler Society,* edited by Sherene Razack. Toronto: Between the Lines.

___. 2015. *Dying from Improvement: Inquests and Inquiries into Indigenous Deaths in Custody.* Toronto: University of Toronto Press.

Renais, Alain, dir. *Night and Fog.* 1955; France. Black & White 1.37:1, Spine #197.

Riley, Randolph, and El Jones. 2020. "Many a Thousand Gone." In *Until We Are Free: Reflections on Black Lives Matter in Canada,* edited by Rodney Diverlus, Sandy Hudson, and Syrus Ware. Regina: University of Regina Press.

Roach, E.M. 2012. *The Flowering Rock: Collected Poems 1938–1974.* Leeds: Pepal Tree Press.

Rohlehr, Gordon. 1972. "Forty Years of Calypso." *Tapia* 2, 2.

Rutland, Ted. 2018. *Displacing Blackness: Planning, Power, and Race in Twentieth-Century Halifax.* Toronto: University of Toronto Press.

Sanchez, Sonia. 2018. "Haiku and Tanka for Harriet Tubman." Poetry Foundation, April. https://www.poetryfoundation.org/poetrymagazine/poems/146231/haiku-and-tanka-for-harriet-tubman

Sapers, Howard. 2014. "A Case Study of Diversity in Corrections: The Black Inmate Experience in Federal Penitentiaries." *OCI*. https://www.oci-bec.gc.ca/cnt/rpt/oth-aut/oth-aut20131126-eng.aspx

Sexton, Genevieve. 2003. "The Last Witness: Testimony and Desire in Zora Neale Hurston's *Barracoon*." *Discourse* 25, 1–2.

Sharpe, Christina. 2012. "Response to 'Ante-Anti-Blackness.'" *Lateral 1*. https://csalateral.org/section/theory/ante-anti-blackness-response-sharpe/#fnref-2128-10

Simpson, Leanne Betasamosake. 2017. *As We Have Always Done: Indigenous Freedom through Radical Resistance*. Minneapolis: University of Minnesota Press.

Smith, Dorothy. 1987. *The Everyday World as Problematic*. Toronto: University of Toronto Press.

___. 1990. *The Conceptual Practices of Power*. Toronto: University of Toronto Press.

Spillers. Hortense J. 1987. "Mama's Baby, Papa's Maybe: An American Grammar Book." *Diacritics* 17, 2.

___. 2017. "Shades of Intimacy: Women in the Time of Revolution." Lecture delivered at Barnard Center for Research on Women. New York: Barnard College. https://bcrw.barnard.edu/videos/hortense-spillers-shades-of-intimacy-women-in-the-time-of-revolution/

Spivak, Gayatri. 1990. *The Post-Colonial Critic: Interviews, Strategies, Dialogues*, edited by Sarah Harasym. New York: Routledge.

Stoler, Ann Laura. 2006. "Intimidations of Empire: Predicaments of the Tactile and Unseen." In *Haunted by Empire: Geographies of Intimacy in North American History*, edited by Ann Laura Stoler. Durham: Duke University Press.

Tetrault, Justin E.C., Sandra M. Bucerius, and Kevin D. Haggerty. 2020. "Multiculturalism Under Confinement: Prisoner Race Relations Inside Western Canadian Prisons." *Sociology* 54, 3.

Toronto Abolition Convergence. 2020. "An Indigenous Abolitionist Study Guide." *Yellowhead Institute*. https://yellowheadinstitute.org/2020/08/10/an-indigenous-abolitionist-study-group-guide/

Waiser, Bill. 1995. *Park Prisoners: The Untold Story of Western Canada's National Parks, 1914–1946*. Markham: Fifth House Publishing.

Walcott, Rinaldo. 2003. *Black Like Who? Writing Black Canada*, vol. 2, rev. ed. Insomniac Press.

Waldron, Ingrid. 2018. *There's Something in the Water: Environmental Racism in Indigenous and Black Communities*. Halifax: Fernwood Publishing.

Ware, Syrus, and Giselle Dias. 2020. "Revolution and Resurgence: Dismantling the Prison Industrial Complex through Black and Indigenous Solidarity." In *Until We Are Free: Reflections on Black Lives Matter in Canada*, edited by Rodney Diverlus, Sandy Hudson, and Syrus Marcus Ware. Regina: University of Regina Press.

Wesley, Gloria. 2019. *Righting Canada's Wrongs. Africville: An African Nova Scotian Community Is Demolished — and Fights Back*. Halifax: Lorimer and Company.

Wilde, Oscar. 2018. "The Ballad of Reading Gaol." In *The Annotated Prison Writings of Oscar Wilde*, edited by Nicholas Frankel. Cambridge: Harvard University Press.

Woolf, Virginia. 1927. *To the Lighthouse*. Richmond: Hogarth Press.

Wright, Robert Seymour. 2016. "R. v. 'X' and the Advent of Cultural Assessments in Criminal Court." Robert S. Wright, personal website, Sept 14. http://site-vnuty-j3m.dotezcdn.com/uploads/6021F03A3CB994A4.pdf?v=220806012710

Acknowledgements

This book would not be possible without my mother Gwyneth, who will not like that I wrote about her; my mother in the movement Lynn Jones, who teaches me what I know about organizing; and the courage of all the prisoners, deportees, and those facing injustice. To my father, sister, brother, and all my family, who taught me love. To Fatuma, Santina, and all mothers fighting for a better world. Thank you to the Writers' Trust of Canada, who paid for my time in Banff where the first draft of this book was written and to Leanne for making that happen. Thank you to Arts Nova Scotia for the commissioning grant. To Reed for his steadfast love. To Randy, Jerry, Mo, Abdoul, all my students, all those who have endlessly shaped me. To the African Nova Scotian community who nurture me. To all named and unnamed in this book, without whose stories, we would not know. To Lisa, whose supervision gave me academic life back. To Tim, who supported my writing at the *Halifax Examiner* where some of this work first appeared. To Todd for all the history support and stalwart friendship, and to Grisha for all her work and for keeping me organized. To Claire for compiling everything. To Desmond, Idil, Robyn, Harsha, Aisha B., Beverly, Justin, Meenakshi, Ben, Martha, Trevor, Pam, Martin, Donya, Rebecca, Suzanne, Darius, Sakura, Masuma, Rajean, Amina, Aisha A., Robin, Tari, Harry, Jenn, Hanna, Sheila, Adelina, Amanda, Isaac, Asaf, Kim, Joey, Sara, Emma, Ashley, Annie, Rachel, OmiSoore, Benita, Val, Ardath, Ajay, Alex, and all I have organized with, whose names would take pages. Please write your own name on these pages. And to Fazeela, without whom there would be no editing, for her patience, generosity, and brilliance.

Index